HIGH

A PEAK
GUID
N

"A WORLD OF DIFFERENCE"

New England Cartographics, Inc.

Table of Contents

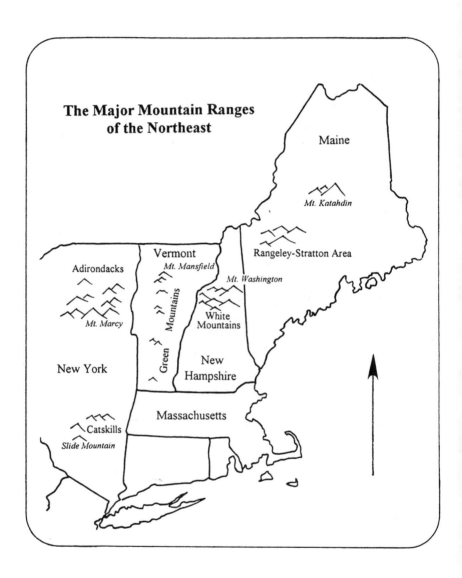

The Major Mountain Ranges
of the Northeast

Maine

Mt. Katahdin

Rangeley-Stratton Area

Vermont

Mt. Mansfield

Mt. Washington

Adirondacks

White
Mountains

Mt. Marcy

Green Mountains

New
Hampshire

New York

Massachusetts

Catskills

Slide Mountain

Preface

Northern New England and New York State contain some of the most striking mountain scenery east of the Rockies. A handful of summits are known to many people; many others are known only to a few. Factual information about both popular and lesser known summits is available but it is spread out over a large number of publications, many of which cover material that extends well beyond the focus of this book. The purpose of this guide is to consolidate into one volume the most relevant information on the topic, to provide readers with some guidance towards other publications and, hopefully, interest users of the mountains in club membership, trail work and resource protection. This book is a directory and resource guide; it is not intended to be the final word on the subject. Readers are encouraged throughout to do additional reading and to acquire specific guidebooks and maps that will allow for safer and more enjoyable adventures in the mountains of the Northeast.

The mountains of the Northeast are perilously close to many major population centers and, as such, they are subject to overuse and abuse. While no formal study has been done, it is clear to many of us out there that most hikers do not start out as peakbaggers. Most seem to spend time exploring and only then develop an interest in climbing specific peaks. In other words, it is doubtful that this publication will bring crowds to the mountains. More likely, it will serve to better inform and organize those already involved.

It should be mentioned here, at the very beginning, that there is a major work available on the mountains of the Northeast and their history that is highly recommended to anyone interested in this subject. The book is "Forest and Crag: A History of Hiking, Trail Blazing, and Adventure in the Northeast Mountains" by Laura and Guy Waterman. This very large book contains fascinating stories about early and more recent climbers and their experiences in this region. While it is not a guidebook, reading it will make any trip to the mountains far more interesting and meaningful.

Acknowledgements

The author would like to thank the following people for their contributions, suggestions and help in the making of this book. Thanks to Chris Ryan who came up with the idea for the project in the first place.

His constant support and material help has been invaluable. Gene Daniell, Neil Zimmerman and Stella Green, all veteran peakbaggers, kindly read the manuscript, caught errors, raised issues and made many excellent suggestions. Valerie Vaughan cleaned up the text, organized the maps and provided valuable format and map-making advice. Thanks also to Tom Berrian, Mark Feller, Brett Gordon and the ADK for their photo submissions.

Vista from Osceola, White Mountains, NH

chapter 1

The Mountains of Northeastern United States

The Appalachian Mountains of Eastern North America run roughly southwest to northeast inland from and parallel to the Atlantic coast. The Appalachians are composed of three parallel ranges. Along the easternmost (and highest) range runs the 2,200-mile Appalachian Trail. To the south, in Georgia, Tennessee, North Carolina and Virginia, the range is called the Blue Ridge and it frequently attains elevations of over 4,000 feet. Forty summits are said to be over 6,000 feet. Great Smoky Mountains National Park is located in the heart of this very mountainous region and Shenandoah National Park towards its northern section. North of Virginia the elevations of the Appalachian chain settle down to under 3,000 feet. The ranges of Maryland, Pennsylvania and New Jersey are a low midpoint between the southern and northern Appalachians.

In New York elevations once again exceed 4,000 feet. The Catskill Mountains, a northern extension of the Allegheny Plateau, contain two summits over 4,000 feet and five over 1,200 meters. The Adirondacks, nearby but technically not part of the Appalachian Mountains, have more than forty over 4,000 feet and two over 5,000. The main spine of the Blue Ridge, which had dipped so low in Pennsylvania, New Jersey and New York, rises again in Massachusetts and Vermont, reaching elevations over 4,000 feet once again in the latter state. More complex mountain building in New Hampshire and Maine has left many summits over this figure; ten over 5,000 feet and one (Mt. Washington) over 6,000. The northernmost high peak is Mt.Katahdin in northern Maine, the focus of the last big surge of the Northeastern Mountains, and a big one indeed. It is fitting that the northern terminus of the Appalachian Trail is located on this mountain.

The mountains of New York State and New England stand apart in several ways from the southern mountains. While not as many of them are as high as those in the south, they are far rockier, and because of their northern latitude, the highest of them extend well above treeline into an alpine zone. In this way they are distinct from the higher summits of the southern Appalachians which are gentler, more heavily covered with vegetation, and never rise past treeline.

Treeline, the point above which trees cannot grow, is not just a product of altitude; it is mostly a product of extreme weather. In Colorado, treeline is reached at about 11,000 feet. Since many summits there lie well above this elevation, much of the mountain scenery is alpine. In the Northeast, the arctic weather swooping down from northern Canada is so intense that treeline occurs between 4,000 and 5,000 feet. Hikers on Northeastern mountains are therefore able to experience small pieces of alpine landscape without suffering from altitude-related problems. Although Northeastern mountains don't compare with those in the western states in elevation, they do better when general relief is considered. Take Rocky Mountain National Park for example. The highest elevation there is Longs Peak at 14,255 feet. The valleys in the park lie at about 8,000 feet and roads take you as high as 12,000 feet. A glance at a guidebook to hiking in that park shows that most summit climbs require about a 3,000-foot elevation gain. Some demand 4,000, and a few even 5,000 feet of gain. But the Adirondack High Peaks, the Presidential Range in New Hampshire and Katahdin in Maine make similar demands. Many climbs to these summits are in the 3,000-to-4,000-foot range of elevation gain. Granted, Rocky Mountain National Park contains a large number of high summits reachable only after a long hike, and the altitude factor makes these climbs even more difficult, but don't underestimate the challenges of the Northeastern mountains. Readers should note that many deaths have occurred in the mountains of the Northeast during all seasons. The combination of bad weather and exposed mountain terrain is a real killer.

When comparing Northeastern mountains with those in the west, another factor is tree cover. An example of this is the San Francisco Peaks north of Flagstaff Arizona. Comprised of the serrated edge of an ancient volcano, these peaks stand out for miles. They rise from a plateau of around 8,000 feet and reach to over 12,000 feet at Humphrey's Peak, a vertical relief comparable to the Northeast's Presidential Range or Katahdin. The big difference is that you can see the San Francisco peaks from all surrounding areas because there are few trees to block the view. If the vegetation were stripped from the Adirondacks or New Hampshire's White Mountains, the effect would be very dramatic. The dense and deeply rooted vegetation of the Northeast also inhibits erosion which would otherwise sharpen the features of these mountains. Trees grow here because, compared to the dry west, the northeast is a rain forest. Rangers sometimes refer to the White Mountain National Forest (WMNF) as the "Asbestos NF" because of the low fire danger.

Peakbagging and Peakbaggers

Once, standing atop a high summit in the White Mountains with a group of peakbaggers, I pointed to a distant peak and asked its name. The answer I got was "That's Mt. Field, you can climb it -- it's over 4,000 feet." I suppose there are two things that can be said about this response. First, here was someone who knew the mountain landscape well, and second, there was apparently a sharp distinction between individual mountains based on elevation that determined whether or not you would or should go there. Anyway, this simple remark said a lot about peakbagging and peakbaggers to me and stimulated my thinking on the subject.

Peakbagging is the activity (some would say sport, others a religion) that involves climbing all the peaks over a specific elevation in a specific area. It's a type of superhiking; goal-oriented like hiking the entire Appalachian Trail, but also a lot like collecting. It motivates people to do some things that they might not otherwise do, and it gives them a sense of accomplishment and reward. There are few rules to follow and plenty of room for individual choice. The challenge is not to defeat another person, but to meet the demands of the mountains themselves. It's also addicting. Upon completing a list, many hikers just can't wait to take on the next peakbagging arena.

Peakbagging started in the Adirondacks. In 1918, Bob and George Marshall and Herb Clark decided to climb all the Adirondack summits over 4,000 feet. The surveys then current indicated there were 46 peaks that met this criterion and by 1925 these hikers had accomplished their goal. Twenty years later another 28 climbers had done the same. In the meanwhile, a club had been formed, called the Adirondack Forty-Sixers, which registered climbs and handed out patches and scrolls to those who had met the challenge. In the next twenty years a total of 343 persons climbed the 46. During 1991 the 3,000th recorded person finished the round. Each of these determined hikers had climbed the original 46 peaks at their own pace in their own chosen order. Meanwhile, a more recent survey had revealed that four of these peaks (Blake, Cliff, Nye and Couchsachraga) measured lower than 4,000 feet. To make matters worse, this particular survey found McNaughton to be higher than originally measured -- it now registered at 4,000 feet exactly. So why weren't the rules of the game changed when the facts changed? Because *climbing the 46* had become a tradition, even a religious quest of sorts. Bob Marshall had gone on to become a major figure in American mountain travel and wilderness protection and the Forty-Sixers were essentially following his

Top: Maine's Mt. Katahdin: the Knife Edge   Photo by Thomas R. Berrian
Bottom: The south slope of Gothics in the Adirondacks

lead. For these and whatever other reasons the new survey changes were ignored.

The desire to bag peaks spilled over to the White Mountains. During the 1950's, an Appalachian Mountain Club (AMC) committee was formed to orchestrate the climbing of all the peaks in the White Mountains measured at over 4,000 feet. Astoundingly, it turned out that there were also 46 peaks that met this condition. As with the Adirondack Forty-Sixers, an official listing and patch was given to those who climbed all of them. Newer surveys also disrupted the White Mountain list, however, and over the years two additional mountains (Galehead in 1975 and Bondcliff in 1982) joined the list, making the total count 48. This was no problem for the pragmatic New Englanders; they just climb two more peaks now.

The psychology of many peakbaggers is such that upon completion of one list, they look for another one, or for a variation on the first. In other words, the activity is just too satisfying to give up -- the process has become the goal. One of the first variations was to climb the list in winter. This is really quite a challenge, especially in the Adirondacks where many peaks have no official trails, and yet this goal has been met by a large number of hardy souls. (Incidentally, winter for peakbaggers means the period from the precise moment of the winter solstice to the same of the vernal equinox.) Another variation was to rearrange components of the list, for example to tackle the five 4,000-footers in Vermont and the twelve in Maine. Two new lists were possible here; the original 63 New England 4,000-footers and, adding New York State, the Northeast 111 (63 New England + 46 Adirondack + 2 Catskill Peaks = 111). Of course, this list included the four Adirondack peaks that have now been surveyed as under 4,000 feet but it didn't include the two new White Mountain 4,000-footers. Today's list brings the total of peaks to 113, or 109 actually over 4,000 feet (MacNaughton isn't counted because it isn't on the original list. Also, it appears to have "shrunk" below the magic number again in a recent survey). Another variation proposed and executed by New England peakbaggers is the New England Hundred Highest Peaks. Here the magic 4,000-foot figure disappears and a more serious ranking enters. It turns out from a recent survey that the lowest of the hundred highest (Mt. Coe in Maine) has an elevation of 3,764 feet. Apparently not yet tired, some dedicated climbers in New England set a 3,000-footer goal, compiled a list, and soon completed the job.

Meanwhile, down in the Catskills where there are only two peaks over 4,000 feet, the Catskill 3500 Club was formed requiring those seeking entry to climb 34 summits over 3,500 feet -- including four of them also in winter. Recently, hikers pointed out that Southwest Hunter should be considered a separate peak and that its inclusion in the list would bring the number of summits to 35 making a neat 35 peaks over 3,500 feet. They were successful in their promotion for this change in the requirements.

Fortunately, mountains don't grow much in a lifetime, so we should be nearing the end of new peakbagging lists in the Northeast very soon. But the "activity" has caught on. In the Mountains of Southeastern U.S. there are 40 peaks over 6,000 feet that hikers aspire to climb. The club that makes the rules there is the "South Beyond 6000' Club." In Colorado are 54 peaks over 14,000 feet. Climbing all of them is known as the "Grand Slam." There are also a number of people who climb the highest point in every state, a project which ranges from a car drive in Florida to a most difficult summit attempt in Alaska.

There are some important and generally overlooked aspects to all this peak listing. First, what determines that a peak is a peak? Many of the mountains in the Northeast, like many of the mountains in the western states, are simply high points on a ridge. The distinguishing factors are the drop and the distance between peaks. The Adirondack rule is that a peak rises at least 300 feet above the col (or saddle) between it and the next peak, or that it lies at least .75 miles distant. The AMC rule is that a peak rises at least 200 feet above the col between it and the next peak. Obviously there is disagreement here, so applying one region's rule to the other might change the makeup of the list. The lists in this book respects both these local distinctions.

A second problem has to do with the surveys themselves. Surveying depends on technical instruments, and these have become more sophisticated over time. The earliest measurements of elevation were done with barometers and triangulation. Today, laser transits are able to measure long distances with only fractions of an inch in error. Aerial photography is also used in modern surveys. It seems only logical that the elevations of some mountains would be corrected periodically. Some mountain summits have never been given a specific elevation by the USGS survey gods, they only have a highest contour line. When this is the case, the actual summit could be as much as 19 feet higher (with 20-foot contours). Further, the latest USGS surveys are done with contours of 10 meters, a difference of 32.8 feet between them. There are 14 Adirondack peaks that were calculated in this manner that make their exact elevation (within this 32-foot range) anyone's guess. The fact that this occurs has made the sport/religion of peakbagging all the more interesting. In the case of the Adirondack Forty-Sixers, survey changes have been ignored. Other groups welcome additional peaks and drop others off their lists.

Bondcliff in the White Mountains

Elevation changes brought about by newer surveys have stimulated some interesting responses from dedicated peakbaggers. Mountains that gained a few feet were reported to have "grown," while those that lost some height "shrank." Mountains that reached the magic 4,000-foot figure have been described by peakbaggers as "new." Poor West Tecumseh, a knob on the shoulder of Tecumseh in the White Mountains, was recently found to have a col between it and the main peak that did not meet the criteria. Master peakbagger Eugene S. Daniell III writes humorously that West Tecumseh has "been exposed as an impostor with a shamefully inadequate col." On the other hand, opponents of peakbagging have equally animated comments about the mountains. Daniel Doan complains that peakbaggers climb North Twin in the White Mountains as a side trip from South Twin, a mile to the south. He says (almost as if the mountain cared), "North Twin is its own mountain and deserves special attention." What he implies is that the trail to North Twin is a good one and worth the effort -- but if you go up this way and then walk over to South Twin, would that mountain be offended?

In putting together this directory, the author has chosen a limiting figure of 1,200 meters which is about 3,937 feet. This accomplishes several purposes. First, it adds another figure to consider in regard to a mountain's elevation, thereby creating a new list. Second, it adopts the metric system by selecting a memorable round number that closely approximates the magic 4,000- foot standard. Third, it works well in the Adirondacks because it brings the total of peaks over this new elevation standard back to 46. In this book the criteria for the listing are that the mountain (1) be in New York State or New England, (2) that it have a summit of 1,200 meters or more as designated by those who decide what exactly is a summit in their area, *or* (3) that it has long been on an important peakbagging list. If these criteria serve to confound established sacred traditions, all the more fun.

Peakbagging will probably always have its enthusiasts and its detractors because many of those who really love the mountains are outspoken, rugged individualists with strong opinions (the demands of walking uphill on a muddy and rocky trail with a weight on your back will do this to you). Arguments can be made in support of peakbaggers by citing the trail work and maintenance contributions that The Adirondack Forty-Sixers have done, as well as their efforts to reseed alpine summits that were suffering from excessive hiking boot trampling. Laura and Guy Waterman, authors and peakbaggers, are recognized for their efforts to improve conditions on the Franconia Ridge in the White Mountains. The first official peakbagger, Bob Marshall, founded the Wilderness Society. Arguments against peakbaggers usually include complaints that they rush through nature and miss the subtleties, or that too many people on the peaks spoils them for others. Many hikers complain that there are too many people in the mountains, but few include themselves in the objectionable count. The fact is, peakbagging is a touchy subject in some circles. Recommended are the excellent and hilarious discussions on the pros and cons of peakbagging found in books by Guy and Laura Waterman, *Forest and Crag*, *Wilderness Ethics* and also *Backwoods Ethics* (recently revised), listed in the bibliography.

Climbing mountains can be seen as a kind of quest. Peakbagging generally attracts individuals who are self-disciplined, determined, serious and often spiritually-oriented (though many wouldn't admit this and work hard at playing it down). A steady ascent of a steep slope can generate a meditative state in which the mind settles into a rhythmic chant while the body plugs on. Long distance runners experience what has been called the "runner's high," and in this regard, so do hikers. During a strenuous and prolonged assault on a high mountain, there is probably a change in brain chemistry that alters consciousness. After this, the arrival at the summit can be amazingly satisfying. Unlike real life, where goals are often intangible or constantly changing, the mountain is *really there*. The summit is attained with both mind and body. Beyond this is the experience of nature. The mountains are overpowering, the vistas awesome; the weather can be placid one hour and deadly the next. In short, peakbaggers can place themselves in environments that put their lives into perspective. Nature is simply bigger than us domesticated primates; it outlasts us. Another "spiritual" thing I've noticed about many of the peakbaggers I've met is their good sense of humor; a trait that is lacking in some of their detractors. Many peakbaggers know how ridiculous their passion is and have learned to laugh at themselves. If one looks at climbing as (1) a kind of meditation that stops the internal dialogue, (2) an overwhelming experience of nature that promotes loss of self-importance and widens one's perspective on life, and (3) a quest of sorts with a goal, then peakbagging/mountain hiking could be said to be a unique spiritual activity.

Hiking and Climbing the Peaks of the Northeast

While this book is *not* intended to be an instruction manual on how to hike and climb, a few suggestions should be made. First, join a club. Whether you are a beginner or expert, some contact with others of like mind makes for a better, safer experience. Membership in a club will keep you informed about the latest changes in trails, rules, regulations, etc. Clubs sponsor group hikes and climbs to the major mountains year-round, they may handle transportation logistics and, in some cases, may even provide some equipment. While guidebooks may provide enough information to get you in and out of the mountains, contact with others who have had some personal experience with an area can often make a big difference. Also, it is not a good idea to go alone on climbs to big mountains in remote areas. Accidents happen; if you are alone, your chances of getting out safely (or even alive) are greatly reduced. Four or more in winter will save a life. Finally, joining a club is also a way of supporting mountain conservation, recreation and trail work.

After joining a club, there are two primary matters regarding hike preparation that should be addressed: the mental and the physical. Mental preparation includes attitude and knowledge. A hiker's attitude toward climbing a mountain is absolutely critical in matters of safety and enjoyment. Hikers should ask themselves why they are putting themselves into a potentially stressful and even dangerous situation. There are plenty of good reasons for climbing mountains, including recreation, exploration, adventure, companionship, personal healing and growth. But reasons such as personal frustration or competition with others need to be examined more closely. Bad attitudes toward crowds or park rangers can lead to poor judgments and trouble. Be flexible and understanding of the rights of others.

Knowledge is the other issue of mental preparation. It is more than just valuable to have knowledge of the goal and the process necessary to

Top: Checking location on a map in the Adirondacks
Bottom: AMC Greenleaf hut just below Mt. Lafayette in the White Mountains

attain it; it can save a life. It is suggested that anyone hiking on the mountains listed in this directory study the terrain ahead of time by consulting the available guidebooks and maps recommended in the text. It is also suggested that they use at least two of the listed maps in finding routes because maps vary -- a second map will often supply a critical detail or simply confirm something vaguely suggested on the first map. Besides knowledge of the terrain, knowledge of how to handle emergencies is extremely important. Don't underestimate the mountains, especially in exposed areas, in winter or during storms. Unexpected bad weather even during summer in areas above treeline can be deadly. Know what to do if accidents occur, as they will from time to time.

Physical preparation includes the condition of both your physical body and the equipment you bring along. It goes without saying that you must be in good physical condition to climb any of the mountains listed in this book. The best way to get in shape is to hike regularly in mountainous areas. If you live near a park where there is only a 300' elevation gain to a low summit, do it several times. Your legs will need to adjust to uphill hiking with a pack on your back. Other possible alternatives are bicycle, exercise bike or x-country ski machine workouts. Don't underestimate the amount of work your body will have to perform when climbing a high peak. Don't attempt a climb if you or any in your party are in questionable shape -- and don't be afraid to bail out and come back another day if you find the hike is too demanding.

Probably the most important piece of equipment needed is boots. These should fit well and be previously broken in. There is nothing so annoying and yet preventable as multiple blisters on your feet. The remedy for this problem is usually "moleskin," available in drugstores, which is cut into pieces and placed over the affected area to prevent further friction and damage. Wearing two pairs of socks can also prevent blister damage. Boots may be made of synthetic materials, thick leather, or, for winter, rubber with leather or plastic tops. The fact that improper selection and adjustment to footwear can ruin your trip cannot be overstated. Don't be overly concerned about fashion because sooner or later your nice new boots will be covered with black mud. The pack is perhaps the second most important piece of equipment. For most summit attempts, a good sized day-pack, about 2,000 to 2,500 cubic inches in volume, is sufficient. Winter climbers will probably want a slightly larger pack or will tie on extra gear. The pack should be very sturdy, have good straps, with optional adjustments to keep it balanced. Some prefer a pack with pockets, others prefer the more traditional climbing sack which requires some digging to find packed items. It is a good idea to include the following items in your pack for spring, summer and autumn hiking.

1. *First aid kit.* This should include bandages of various sizes, disinfectant, pain-killer medicine, antihistamine, moleskin, insect repellent, balm for sore muscles, balm for chapped lips, sunscreen (even in winter), water purification tablets, and any personal items (such as tampons) or medication that you may need.

2. *Water containers.* Wide-mouth plastic bottles are popular and convenient. Canteens and insulated bottles are also a possibility. The important thing is that the container shouldn't leak in the pack when it is turned upside down. A water filter or iodine tablets are needed if you plan on getting water along the trail. Know how to use your filter and how long to let tablets work. Be aware that water may be scarce in some places or even polluted (usually by other hikers). If you bring your own water from the start bring enough; at least a quart or two for an easy climb, more for the bigger peaks or an overnight. Make sure you drink enough as dehydration can be a serious threat. During winter, an insulating pouch is needed for the water bottle to prevent it from freezing. Many hikers use a heavy wool sock for this purpose. Also, carrying a thermos containing hot liquid is a good idea.

3. *Clothing.* What you wear depends on the season but a layering system should be the basis of your approach to this matter. It is far better to have three or four layers of clothing than one light shirt and one heavy jacket. For warmth, wool is excellent and a wool sweater and cap should be carried when hiking the higher peaks where weather can change abruptly at any time of year. Unlike cotton, wool will also keep you warm when wet. Today a number of synthetic fabrics, such as polypropelene, pile and fleece, offer lightweight and comfortable protection for hikers. Some of these are quite expensive, but certainly worth knowing about. Visit an outfitter store to learn about what is available. A Gore-Tex (R) parka and rain pants will allow your body to breath, yet will keep you dry in the rain. This dual function is not the case with vinyl plastic or coated nylon. Hiking a long distance with these can be hot and sweaty -- you'll get wet in spite of your protection. For the exposed summits, a parka shell can also serve as a windbreaker. Don't forget sunglasses, a hat, a bandana, gloves and an extra pair of socks in case your feet get wet.

4. *Food.* Besides water, your body will need energy. Fruit, a sandwich and other snacks will be adequate for day hikes. Your body will need high energy food; many hikers eat candy bars and foods containing high levels of carbohydrates. Others prefer more natural sources of sugar such as raisins and dried fruit. GORP (Good Old Raisins and Peanuts) is popular; many hikers also add M & M's to the mix.

5. *Gadgets and Tools.* Under this category are: compass, flashlight, penknife, altimeter, pocket binoculars, and a camera. Be sure you know how to use a map and compass. Flashlights, or better still, a headlamp, can be very useful when nightfall comes sooner than you want it to. Bring one on every hike.

6. *Miscellaneous gear.* A piece of closed-cell foam pad makes a dry, warm and comfortable seat during breaks. A small plastic trowel is handy for digging discreet "bathroom" holes. A small towel and/or bandana will often come in handy.

Winter demands more of everything. You will need some additional special equipment and probably additional training. In order to travel over ice and snow you will need insulated boots, snowshoes and crampons. The matter of which kind of boots to wear is an important decision. Many winter hikers prefer traditional rubber/leather boots with felt liners. More technically minded climbers may prefer a more complex, and expensive, boot. Winter boots must be able to fit into snowshoes and crampons. The type of snowshoes appropriate for climbing peaks on packed-snow trails are those that sport a hinged binding with crampon-like claws or, preferably, a more traditional crampon. These are typically made of aircraft aluminum with neoprene webbing -- and they are expensive. The hinge will allow you to move up steep slopes far more easily than you could with more traditional snowshoes (which are best suited for deep snow on flat terrain). Crampons are necessary for hiking over ice and are helpful when following trails that have been compacted by previous hikers. Twelve-point crampons are the standard, though some hikers will use lighter four- point instep crampons in places where they are adequate to insure stability and grip. Please take winter hiking and climbing very seriously, and prepare for possible problems on your trip.

How To Use This Guidebook

The 124 peaks listed in the following directory are over 1,200 meters (except for Nye and Couchsachraga in the Adirondacks which, although "shrunk" by surveys, are still climbed by aspiring Forty-Sixers). This figure corresponds to 3937 feet. In all cases, this elevation is high enough that the upper reaches of the mountain are well into the northern spruce/fir forests. The higher summits extend beyond treeline and contain alpine areas that support fragile communities of rare plants that do not take well to hiker's boots. When above treeline, please take care to stay on the trail or on the rocks.

This book was written to consolidate material that has been available, but spread out, in many other previous publications. It does not pretend to supersede these other guidebooks, it merely attempts to organize the information and make it more accessible. Readers who have no experience climbing high summits should work up gradually to the challenge by climbing some of the bigger mountains in southern New England like Greylock, Monadnock, Ascutney, or Cardigan, or try some easy ascents in the Adirondacks, Catskills, Green and White Mountains.

The author wishes to make it perfectly clear that this book is designed to provide access to information and does not contain all the answers. The existence of trails up a mountain is noted, but detailed descriptions of trails are to be found in the relevant guidebooks listed. While the length of the various trails to each summit is given, the elevation gain is not. A 2.5 mi. hike with a 3,500 ft. elevation gain is far more strenuous than a 5 mi. hike with the same gain. In some cases a trail will climb more than one summit on its way to the particular summit in the list. The elevation gain in such a situation may be considerable and the hike that much more difficult. The reader is encouraged to consult the maps in order to estimate the elevation gain of any given climb.

Trailheads in the listings may be found by consulting the appropriate guidebooks. These normally give the latest directions for parking areas and notify the reader of any particular rules and regulations. The DeLorme Mapping Company publishes a series of state atlases that will be of great help in finding trailheads. Some well-established parking areas are shown on the maps in this book but there are many others, subject to change, that the user will find listed in the relevant guidebooks.

The maps in this book are based on United States Geological Survey (USGS) maps. Some of them are old, out-of-date publications and many have been reduced to fit the book's trim size. We have chosen to use them to give the reader a two-dimensional view of each summit. Although the routes of major trails, shelters and parking areas have been added as an overlay, they are not designed to be used as a single field reference.

The scales of the maps in this book vary considerably; study the scale diagram on each map to judge distances. USGS maps cover sections of land called quadrangles, or "quads," based on latitude and longitude. These come in two main sizes; 15' (' = minute) and 7.5.' The 15' series covers an area measuring 15'x 15' or one sixteenth of a square degree of both latitude and longitude. The 7.5' series covers one quarter of a 15' series map, or one sixty-fourth of a square degree of latitude and longitude. 15' minute maps are smaller scale maps which show greater area in less detail. 7.5' maps are larger scale which show a smaller area, but in much greater detail. USGS maps are published with dates and periodically revised, through aerial photography. Newer structures that didn't exist when the original survey was first done are sometimes later added, often printed in purple. Also, as has already been noted, elevations are often revised as well. In spite of all this, the general topography almost always remains the same. Recently, the U.S. Geological Survey has changed the format of some of these maps noting elevations in meters and offering a choice of folded or flat maps. See the appendix in this book for ordering information. This book's maps are black & white photographs of the different scale USGS maps noted above. The cartographer added trail information in dashed and dotted lines. Some (but not all) shelters, parking areas, etc., are noted with a symbol. In many cases the proper trail is accurately printed on the base map so the dashed line is simply used for

Vista from the Blackhead Range in the Catskills

Taking a break on the way to a summit

emphasis. In other cases, a trail is shown on the USGS base map but its exact route is no longer accurate due to error or, more likely, a trail relocation. In this case, the trail symbols that have been drawn represent the correct route and the reader should ignore the route of the trail as it may be printed on the base map.

The mountains of the Northeast are experiencing rapid development; particularly tourist-based such as ski areas, condos, and second homes. Much of this recent development does not appear on the base maps that were used to compile this book. Always remember, there are many more roads, houses, resorts, and even trails that are not shown on these maps. While the USGS-based maps accompanying the peak descriptions were drawn as accurately as possible, they should not be used as a sole source of information in the field. Maps differ; one will show something that another will omit. It is recommended that at least one of the other maps, and preferably two, listed in the directory be obtained and used with this book before any summit is attempted. Also recommended is a current road atlas of the general area you wish to visit.

Each summit in the directory has its own unique properties. While some peaks are dramatic and offer outstanding vistas, others provide more subtle experiences. Readers are encouraged to study a peak by examining maps and reading guidebook descriptions before attempting a climb. Knowledge of water sources, interesting rock formations, waterfalls or alternate trails can make a great difference in overall enjoyment of a trip -- and it may even save a life.

Most of the mountains in this directory are located on public land administered by a state or federal agency. Each park or forest has its own set of rules and regulations that may change somewhat over the years as visitor use increases or declines. Below is a list of guidelines that anyone exploring the mountains listed in this guide should respect. They may not apply perfectly to each park or forest, but they will give you an idea of what to expect when entering such an area. Current conditions and rules and regulations are usually posted at park or forest headquarters or ranger stations. Make an inquiry about the rules and regulations before attempting a climb or overnight outing.

Hiking Safety Rules

1. Hike with a group, but not with more than 10 persons (this is a general rule, check local regulations before doing anything). Too many people detracts from the enjoyment of nature and may even cause damage. Hiking alone may be risky. Make your plans known to others before embarking on a climb. Let the rangers know what you are planning to do. Park at designated areas. Trailhead car vandalism is becoming a problem in some areas. Lock your car but leave your glove compartment open to show possible thieves you have nothing to offer them. Sign in at any trail registers. Obtain a hiking permit if one is required.

2. Overuse of the mountains has become a problem. Help cut down on hiker impact by avoiding the more popular areas on weekends. Consider midweek and off-season hiking as an option, or explore the lesser known peaks.

2. Wear appropriate clothing, carry the essentials and be prepared for weather changes and emergencies. Know how to use a map and compass.

3. Keep track of all members in your group. Make clear plans if you need to separate during the hike. Don't let the inexperienced separate from the more experienced and don't let anyone push themselves to the point of exhaustion. It's better to turn back than ask for trouble.

4. Respect the fragility of alpine summits. Walk only on the marked trail or keep on the rocks so as not to damage the rare plant species that live there.

5. Camp at least 200 feet from trails and water sources. Do not camp at higher elevations, usually over 4,000 feet (check for local rules on this).

Use a portable stove rather than a wood fire to cook. Respect camp fire regulations. Do not wash with soap in water sources. Dig a small trench or hole well away from water sources for human waste. Cover with leaf litter and dirt.

Happy Hiking!

Leaving the summit of Mt. Skylight in the Adirondacks

Chapter 2

The Granite Mountains of Maine

Maine Geology

With the exception of Vermont's Green Mountains, which are a long distinct chain, the mountains of northern New England follow no definite pattern and appear to be randomly distributed, particularly so in Maine. As in New Hampshire, many Maine mountains are composed of granite, an igneous (volcanic) rock, or of metamorphic rock (rocks transformed by heat and pressure). Mountain building was a complicated process here; what we see today is only the latest topography in a long history of changes.

When continental plates collide, as they once did when the Appalachian Mountains were formed, the effects can be varied. Some portions of the edges of the plates were pushed up, others pushed down towards the heat of the earth's interior where melting occurred. Some of this molten rock was returned to the surface as lava, but some cooled slowly deep beneath the Earth's surface, as far as 9 miles below, forming large domes. This is how crystalline granite is formed. As the land rose (what geologists call uplifting), the erosive forces of wind, water and ice on the surface cut into the upper layers of rock and eventually exposed these great domes (plugs) of granite. It is due to the hardness and resistance to erosion that this granite is still standing as mountains.

Granite mountains in Maine include Mt. Katahdin, Saddleback and The Horn. Sugarloaf is formed of gabbro, similar to granite but with a slightly different mineral composition. Mount Bigelow is made from sedimentary rocks that came into contact with molten rock. This situation causes a hardening of the sedimentary rocks which creates metamorphic rock, and in this case, schists and gneisses.

About 65 million years ago the surface of Maine was a smooth plain. About 25 million years ago an uplift occurred and erosion began in earnest. The present landscape came into being because this erosion was uneven; the soft rock was removed, leaving the most resistant rock masses (mostly granite) as mountains. About one million years ago changes in the Earth's climate caused a cooling trend in the polar regions where snowfalls didn't melt, but accumulated. Eventually this ice pack extended like a huge glacier pressing down over the northern part of North America, completely covering New England. As this mass of ice moved over the mountains (it covered them by thousands of feet), it scoured off vegetation, reducing surfaces to bare rock. Today, the bare summits of the higher mountains still show the effects of glaciation, even after the last retreat of ice some 12,000 years ago. The glacial ice mass also rounded out river valleys and ravines, dug out shallow areas (creating lakes), and moved huge boulders (called erratics), depositing them further south, far from their original location.

The Ice Age was not just one huge ice mass mowing down everything in its path. Prior to and following the time that the main continental glacier had covered everything, individual "mountain" glaciers formed on some of the higher peaks. In a cool climate where snowfall exceeds the melt, mountain snow and ice accumulates over the years and begins to move downhill in the direction that is steepest and offers least resistance. Glaciers are formed by this method, and once in motion, they carve out the depression or ravine that they follow. Glacially carved ravines are called cirques, named because they are rounded (circular in a sense). There are dramatic cirques on Mt. Katahdin (Great Basin) and also on Crocker Mountain. Lakes which are often found at the bottom of a cirque are called tarns. A good example is Chimney Pond at the base of Mt. Katahdin.

Hiking Clubs in Maine

The Appalachian Mountain Club (AMC), the oldest American hiking club and largest in the Northeast, publishes the *Maine Mountain Guide*. This indispensable book contains descriptions of hiking trails and current information on trail relocations, rules and regulations. The AMC also publishes maps of the Katahdin area and the Rangeley-Stratton area which come with the Maine Mountain Guide or may be purchased separately. The Maine chapter of the AMC organizes hikes and climbs throughout the year.

The Maine Appalachian Trail Club (MATC) is specifically concerned with the Appalachian Trail in Maine. It was founded in 1935 by Myron H. Avery, one of the creators of the Appalachian Trail. Since that time the MATC has built, maintained and relocated miles of trail in Maine. This has been no easy feat as Maine has more true wilderness than any of the other states that the AT passes through. The MATC is composed of both individuals and organizations, including the AMC and other outdoor clubs.

Katahdin: The Tableland   *Photo by Thomas R. Berrian*

Since the Appalachian Trail climbs or passes near almost all of the higher summits in Maine, the MATC guidebook, *Guide to the Appalachian Trail in Maine,* is quite useful. With the guidebook comes a set of seven excellent color maps that include an elevation profile of the section covered and detailed trail information. This valuable guidebook is published in cooperation with the Appalachian Trail Conference (ATC) which oversees the entire 2,200 mile Appalachian Trail that runs from Springer Mountain in Georgia to Maine's Mt. Katahdin.

Management Agencies and Land Ownership

The Katahdin region (Baxter, Hamlin and North and South Brother) is public land that lies within Baxter State Park. This park has many rules and regulations and access is limited. Write for more information (see under Baxter Peak). Bigelow Mountain (Avery Peak and West Peak) has recently been acquired by the State as the Bigelow Preserve. Old Speck is located in Grafton Notch State Park. The other Maine peaks are owned by ski operators, logging companies, and individuals.

Highest Summits in Maine

Mountain	Elevation: ft/m	Date(s) Climbed
1. Katahdin, Baxter Peak	5267/1605	
2. Katahdin, Hamlin Peak	4751/1448	
3. Sugarloaf	4250/1295*	
4. Old Speck	4180/1274	
5. Crocker	4168/1270	
6. Bigelow, West Peak	4150/1265	
7. North Brother	4143/1263	
8. Saddleback	4116/1255	
9. Bigelow, Avery Peak	4088/1246	
10. Abraham	4049/1234	
11. Saddleback, The Horn	4023/1226	
12. South Crocker	4010/1222*	
13. Spaulding	3988/1215	
14. Readington, North Peak	3984/1214	
15. Snow	3960/1207	
16. South Brother	3960/1207	

Elevations based on contour intervals from latest USGS maps. Source: AMC White Mountain Guide.

Katahdin from Chimney Pond   *Photo by Thomas R. Berrian*

DIRECTORY OF HIGH SUMMITS IN MAINE

Katahdin, Baxter Peak (1)

Elevation: 5267 ft./1605 m.
USGS Quad/Coordinates: 15' Mount Katahdin: 45N54/68W55.
Best Maps: DeLorme's Map and Guide of Baxter State Park and Katahdin, AMC: Mount Katahdin and Baxter State Park, MATC Map 1.
Access: Baxter State Park is located about 20 miles northwest of Millinocket, ME and about 80 miles north of Bangor. Campgrounds and trailheads are off Perimeter Road and Roaring Brook Road. Trailheads are located at Katahdin Stream Campground, Abol Campground and Roaring Brook Campground.
Trails to Summit: Several, including the Appalachian Trail (Hunt Trail) which from Katahdin Stream Campground terminates on Baxter Peak (5.2 miles). The Abol Slide Trail leaves Abol Campground and ascends nearly 4,000 ft. in 3.75 miles to Baxter Peak. The Helon Taylor Trail, named for a former supervisor of Baxter State Park, begins near the Roaring Brook Campground and ascends 3,400 ft. to Pamola in about 3.25 miles. From there, the Knife Edge Trail leads in 1.1 mile to the chief summit, Baxter Peak. From the same starting point, the 3.3 mile Chimney Pond Trail climbs to Chimney Pond, a glacial tarn 2,000 ft. directly below the various peaks of Katahdin. From there, Baxter Peak may be reached via the Cathedral (steep: 1.6 miles) or Saddle Trail (easiest: 2.2 miles).
Comments: The terminus of the Appalachian Trail (which starts in Georgia) is Baxter Peak, the highest point of this huge mountain. Katahdin is a very isolated, massive granite mountain with a long curving summit ridge with several summits including Baxter Peak (5,267 ft.), South Peak (5,240 ft.), Pamola (4,902 ft.) and Hamlin (4,751 ft.). Between Baxter Peak and Hamlin Peak the ridge drops several hundred feet, and these two high points are considered separate summits by peakbaggers. Between Baxter Peak and Pamola is the Knife Edge, a long and dangerous section of narrow trail with precipitous drops on either side (not to be attempted by the faint-hearted). North of and below the Knife Edge is the Great Basin, a glacial cirque, with its tarn Chimney Pond. Northwest of Baxter Peak is the "tableland," a flat four-mile stretch of alpine rocks towering over the surrounding forests and lakes.

 The Native American word Katahdin means "greatest mountain." It stands in sharp relief to its surroundings, which to the south and east are only about 400 ft., and to the north, about 1,000 ft. above sea level. The first recorded climb of the mountain was in 1804. Katahdin is a granite pluton, a large roundish mass of pink granite in part buried, part exposed.

  Baxter State Park, created in 1931, was a gift to the State of Maine by former governor Percival P. Baxter. Baxter's conditions regarding this gift were that it be left forever wild as a sanctuary for animals and as a public park for recreational purposes. Today, the park contains over 200,000 acres of mountains, forests and lakes. It is very tightly managed by the State of Maine. Entrance to the park is limited and winter climbing restricted. For current information about reservations, rules and regulations (no dogs), and fees write to Baxter State Park, 64 Balsam Drive, Millinocket, ME 04462. It is wise to write for reservations as early as January for summer hiking.

Katahdin, Hamlin Peak (1)

Elevation: 4751 ft./1448 m.
USGS Quad/Coordinates: 15' Mount Katahdin: 45N56/68W56.
Best Maps: See Katahdin, Baxter Peak.
Access: See Katahdin, Baxter Peak.
Trails to Summit: From Roaring Brook Campground: Chimney Pond Trail, North Basin Trail to Hamlin Ridge Trail (total distance 5.3 miles). Other longer trail combinations are possible from Perimeter Road, e.g. Abol/Hunt Trails to Baxter Cutoff to Northwest Basin Trail.
Comments: Hamlin Peak is part of the Katahdin ridge and is located about 1.5 miles north of Baxter Peak. It is located on the northern part of the curving Katahdin mass, well above treeline.

North Brother (2)

Elevation: 4143 ft./1263 m.
Management agency: Baxter State Park.
USGS Quads/Coordinates: 7.5' Doubletop/7.5' & 15' Mt. Katahdin/15' Harrington Lake: 48N57/68W59.
Best Maps: DeLorme's Map and Guide of Baxter State Park and Katahdin, AMC: Mt. Katahdin and Baxter State Park.
Access: See Katahdin, Baxter Peak.
Trail to Summit: Marston Trail (4 miles).
Comments: North Brother is the highest peak in a range leading

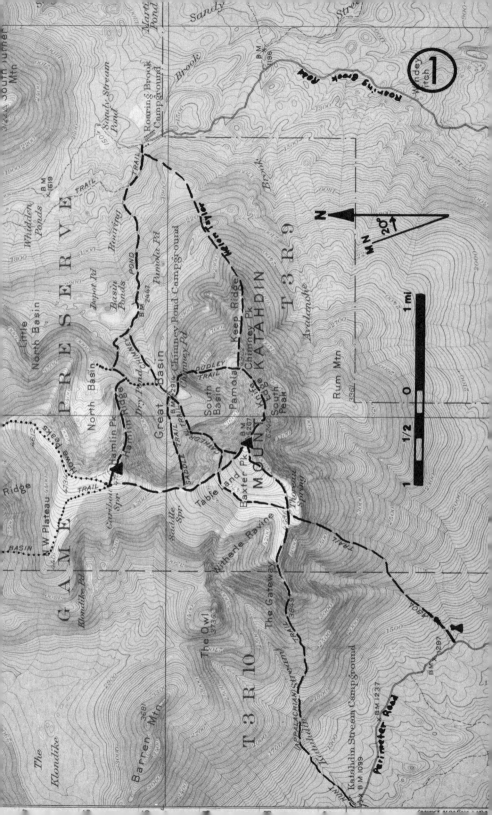

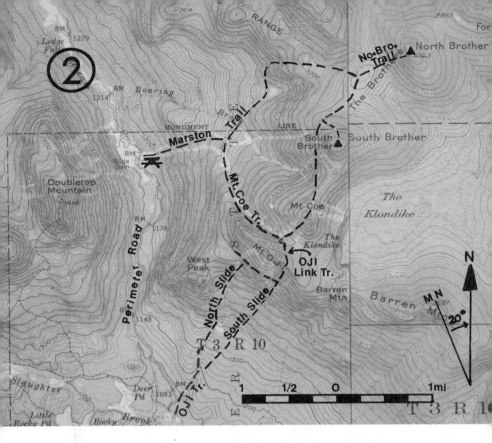

northwest and about seven miles distant from Katahdin. Unlike most of the other high summits in Maine, North and South Brother are not on the Appalachian Trail. The Marston Trail trailhead has been relocated on Perimeter Road near the Slide Dam Picnic Area about six miles north of the Katahdin Stream Campground and Ranger Station. The summit of this remote mountain is bare.

South Brother (2)

Elevation: 3942 ft./1202 m.
USGS Quads/Coordinates: 7.5' Doubletop/7.5' & 15' Mt. Katahdin/15' Harrington Lake: 48N56/69w00.
Best Maps: See North Brother.
Trail to Summit: Marston Trail to South Brother Side Trail (3.8 miles to summit).
Access: From Marston Trail near Slide Dam Picnic Area.
Comments: South Brother is due south of North Brother. The 1-mile trail to its summit, which has a southerly vista, begins in the col between these two peaks about 3 miles from the trailhead. A large slide exists on the western face of this mountain.

Rangeley-Stratton Area

Bigelow, West Peak (3)

Elevation: 4150 ft./1265 m.
USGS Quad/Coordinates: 15' Stratton: 45N09/70W17.
Best Maps: AMC: Rangeley-Stratton map, MATC: Map 5.
Access: From Maine 27, about 4.5 miles southeast of Stratton, to Stratton Brook Road. Also from East Flagstaff Lake Road.
Trails to Summit: Fire Warden's Trail to AT (4 miles), Appalachian Trail northbound (7 miles), Safford Brook Trail to AT (5 miles).
Comments: The 9-mile-long Bigelow Range offers some of Maine's best exposed ridgetop hiking and passes over two peaks above 4,000 feet that lie within a mile of each other. Bigelow is often referred to as Maine's "Second Mountain" (second in overall mass and beauty to Katahdin, though not second highest). It is a huge mountain; hiking from end to end on the Bigelow Range Trail/Appalachian Trail involves an elevation gain of 6,000 ft. This mountain was saved from resort development by concerned citizens; 33,000 acres are now owned by the State. A loop hike that includes both West Peak and Avery Peak is possible using the Horns Pond Trail, the Appalachian Trail and the Fire Warden's Trail, although Avery must be climbed on its own from Bigelow Col. In this col between Avery and West Peak is a trail shelter.

Bigelow, Avery Peak (3)

Elevation: 4088 ft./1246 m.
USGS Quad/Coordinates: 15' Stratton: 45N09/70W16.
Best Maps: AMC: Rangeley-Stratton map, MATC: Map 5.
Access: See Bigelow, West Peak.
Trails to Summit: Fire Warden's Trail to AT (4 miles), Safford Brook Trail to AT (4.2 miles).
Comments: Avery Peak is located less than one mile east of Bigelow's West Peak along the same ridge. It was named for Myron H. Avery, a major force in the creation of the Appalachian Trail, and especially the Maine section. There is an old fire tower on its summit. The views from the bare summit are excellent and on clear days both Katahdin and Mt. Washington are visible. Flagstaff Lake, a reservoir for water power, lies to the north. Be considerate of the fragile alpine vegetation that grows here.

Top: Avery Peak from West Peak   *Photos by Thomas R. Berrian*
Bottom: The Horn on Bigelow Mountain

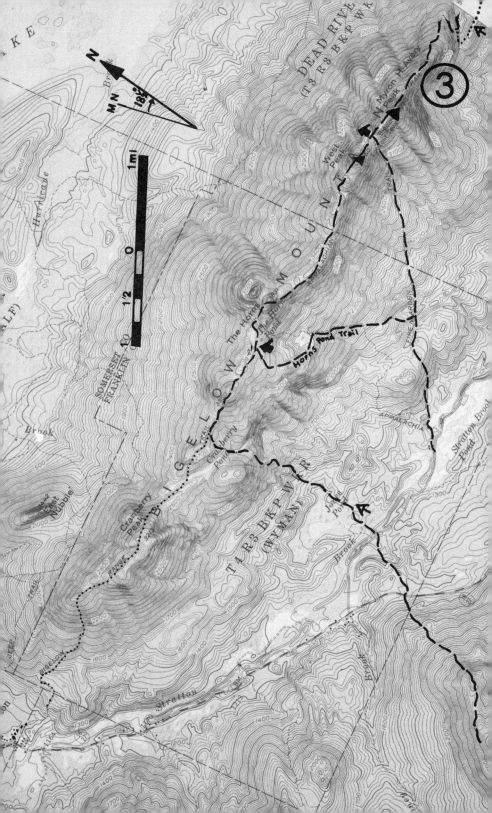

Crocker Mountain, North Peak (4)
See also (5)

Elevation: 4168 ft./1270 m.
USGS Quad/Coordinates: 15' Stratton: 45N03/70W23.
Best Maps: AMC: Rangeley-Stratton map, MATC: Map 6.
Access: From ME 27, 5 miles southeast of Stratton (2.7 miles northwest of Sugarloaf ski area) or via Caribou Valley Road 1 mile northwest of the entrance to Sugarloaf ski area.
Trail to Summit: Appalachian Trail southbound from ME 27 (4.9 miles). AT northbound from Caribou Valley Road (reported to be deteriorating badly as of this writing) over South Crocker 3.1 miles).
Comments: Crocker Mountain, with two peaks over 4,000 ft. in elevation, has on its eastern face a large glacial cirque, evidence that it supported its own glacier at one time. Its northern summit is wooded but offers limited vistas. There is a 380 ft. col between the two peaks which, along with Redington, form the Crocker/Redington Pond Range.

Crocker, South Peak (4) See also (5)

Elevation: 4010 ft./1222 m.
USGS Quad/Coordinates: 15' Stratton: 45N02/70W23.
Best Maps: AMC: Rangeley-Stratton map, MATC: Map 6.
Access: See Crocker Mountain, North Peak.
Trail to Summit: Appalachian Trail.
Comments: South Crocker is located about 1 mile south of Crocker Mountain's North Peak on the Appalachian Trail. An approach from the north requires climbing the north peak first (5.9 miles); an approach from the south climbs steeply from Caribou Valley up Crocker Cirque (2.1 miles). The actual summit, reached via a short side trail, is rockier and offers slightly better views than the north peak.

Redington (4)
See also (5)

Elevation: 3984 ft./1214 m.
USGS Quad: 15' Stratton: 45N01/70W23.
Trail to Summit: none.
Best Maps: AMC: Rangeley-Stratton, MATC: Map 6.
Access: From ME 27 via Appalachian Trail.

Comments: This peak is reachable from South Crocker over which the Appalachian Trail crosses. Other approaches are possible, however. See the AMC 4000 Footer Committee's *Guide to New England Hundred Highest Peaks* for more details.

Sugarloaf (4)
See also (5)

Elevation: 4250 ft./1295 m.
USGS Quad/Coordinates: 15' Stratton: 45N02/70W18.
Best Maps: AMC: Rangeley-Stratton, MATC: Map 6.
Access: From ME 27 via Caribou Valley Road and Appalachian Trail or via the Sugarloaf ski area.
Trails to Summit: Appalachian Trail to South Branch Trail (2.5 miles). A rough road from the ski area, as well as various ski trails, also allows access to the summit.
Comments: Sugarloaf is Maine's second highest mountain. Hikers will prefer climbing the mountain via the AT south of Crocker Mountain where it crosses Caribou Valley Road. There is also a brook crossing here that can be a problem during times of high water. Although the AT only grazes the side of the mountain, the summit may be reached via the blue-blazed Sugarloaf Summit Side Trail. Sugarloaf's summit, which has been developed for skiing and contains communications facilities, offers excellent views. Its location near the center of many 4,000-footers makes the vista particularly dramatic. Ski lifts and a gondola offer an alternative route down the mountain. Sugarloaf is composed of gabbro, formed from the slow cooling of a molten plug of rock like granite, but darker due to the presence of dark minerals.

Spaulding (4)
See also (5)

Elevation: 3988 ft./1216 m.
USGS Quads/Coordinates: 15' Stratton, 15' Phillips: 45N00/70W20.
Best Maps: AMC: Rangeley-Stratton, MATC: Map 6.
Access: From Maine 16/27 via Appalachian Trail.
Trails to Summit: Spaulding's summit is reached via a short spur trail from the Appalachian Trail. From Caribou Valley Road the distance is 4 miles.
Comments: Spaulding lies due south of Sugarloaf Mountain and is connected to it by a ridge. Its wooded summit is closely bypassed by the

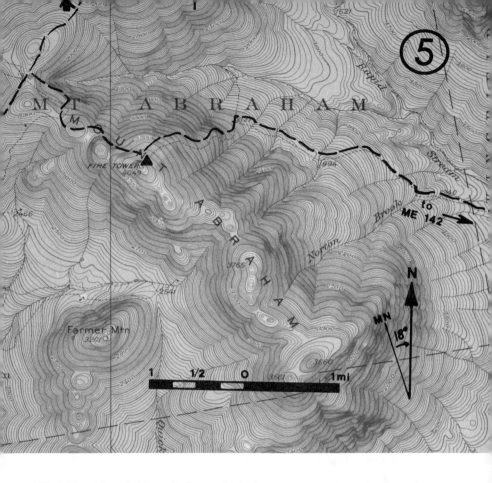

AT. A blue-blazed side trail, from which there are some views, leads to the actual summit.

Abraham (5)

Elevation: 4049 ft./1234 m.
USGS Quads/Coordinates: 7.5' Mt. Abraham, 15' Kingfield, 15' Phillips: 44N58/70W20.
Best Maps: AMC: Rangeley-Stratton map, MATC: Map 6.
Access: via Kingfield and logging roads off ME 142 and 16/27. (See AMC Maine Mountain Guide).
Trails to Summit: The Fire Warden's trail accessible from lumber company roads reaches the summit from the southeast (4.5 miles). The Mt. Abraham Side Trail, a spur trail off the Appalachian Trail, reaches the summit from the north. From Caribou Valley Road this route is 6.6 miles.
Comments: This massive mountain is far from the main roads and requires some moderately rough dirt-road driving to the Fire Warden's

trailhead, or a long 13-mile hike on the AT. An extensive portion of Mt. Abraham's long summit ridge is boulder-strewn (much like the summit of Mount Washington) and above timberline. There is an abandoned fire tower on the summit. The mountain is composed of metamorphic rocks including schists and slates.

Saddleback Mtn. (6)

Elevation: 4116 ft./1255 m.
USGS Quads/Coordinates: 7.5' Saddleback Mountain/Redington, 15' Rangeley/Phillips: 44N56/70W30.
Best Maps: AMC: Rangeley-Stratton map, MATC: Map 6.
Trails to Summit: Appalachian Trail (5.1 miles), Saddleback Trail (from ski area).
Access: From ME 4, 9.9 miles southeast of Rangeley and 2.5 miles northwest of Madrid. Also via the Saddleback Ski Area.
Comments: Saddleback Mountain has two summits over 4,000 ft. located about 1 mile apart (1.6 mi. by trail) on its ridge. The Appalachian Trail runs along the entire ridge connecting the main summit and The Horn. A long stretch of the summit ridge is above treeline and offers excellent views as well as exposure to the elements. Saddleback is composed of granodiorite, a dark granite containing reflective pieces of mica, which was worn to a smooth surface during previous glaciation.

The Saddleback Mountain Ski Area, from which rises the Saddleback Trail (fastest way off the mountain), covers the northern slopes of this mountain. There have been some disputes over additional development near the mountain between the National Park Service, which manages the AT, and the ski area.

Saddleback, The Horn (6)

Elevation: 4023 ft./1226 m.
USGS Quads/Coordinates: 15' Phillips, 15' Rangeley: 44N57/70W29.
Best Maps: AMC: Rangeley-Stratton, MATC: Map 6.
Trail to Summit: Appalachian Trail from ME 4 (6.7 miles).
Access: See Saddleback Mtn.
Comments: Located about 1 mile (1.6 mi. by trail) northeast of Saddleback Mtn., The Horn is a high point on the long Saddleback Mtn. ridge, much of which lies above timberline. Between the two is a col (or saddle) requiring a major descent of at least 500 ft.

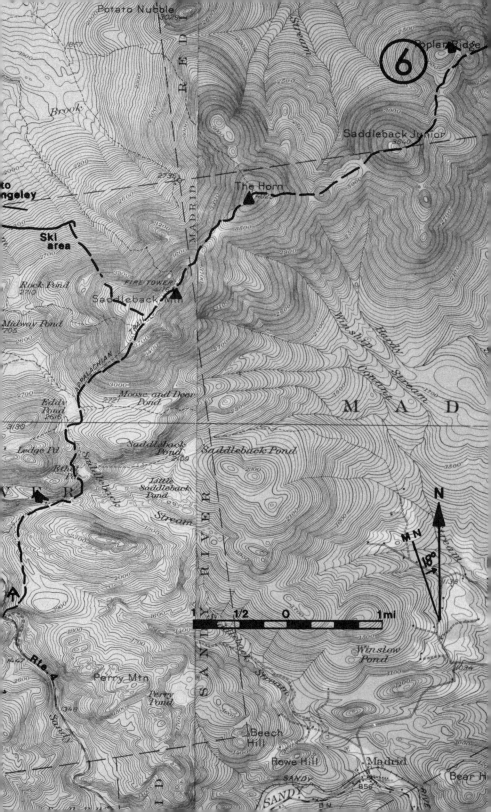

Snow Mountain (7)

Elevation: 3960 ft./1207 m.
USGS Quad/Coordinates: 7.5' Chain of Ponds: 45N17/70W42.
Best Maps: See above.
Trail to Summit: Fire Warden's trail to abandoned fire tower (5 miles).
Access: Complicated. See *AMC Maine Mountain Guide* and the AMC 4000 Footer Committee's *Routes to New England 100 Highest.*
Comments: Remote Snow Mountain is formed of pre-Cambrian gneiss, the oldest rock in Maine. From the summit, on which an abandoned fire tower is located, are sweeping vistas in all directions. Logging is frequent on the mountain and may obscure portions of the trail. This mountain is on land owned by the Penobscot Nation who at one time limited hiker access.

Oxford County

Old Speck (8)

Elevation: 4180 ft./1274 m.
USGS Quad/Coordinates: 15' Old Speck Mountain: 44N34/70W57.
Best Maps: AMC: Carter-Mahoosuc, MATC: Map 7.
Trails to Summit: Old Speck Trail (AT) (3.8 miles). An alternate route utilizes the Link Trail and the East Spur Trail (4.4 miles).
Access: Grafton Notch State Park. From Maine 26 about 15 miles southeast of New Hampshire state line and 2.7 miles northwest of Screw Auger Falls.
Comments: Old Speck, Maine's third highest mountain, is located in Grafton Notch State Park, which is just east of the New Hampshire border. The Old Speck Trail (a part of the Appalachian Trail) leaves Grafton Notch and reaches the flat and wooded summit in under 4 miles. The Link and the East Spur trails (poorly marked in places) offer a somewhat longer, rockier, strenuous but more scenic route to the summit. Grafton Notch, with its 1,000 ft. rock walls that separate Old Speck from Baldpate Mountain, is quite spectacular.

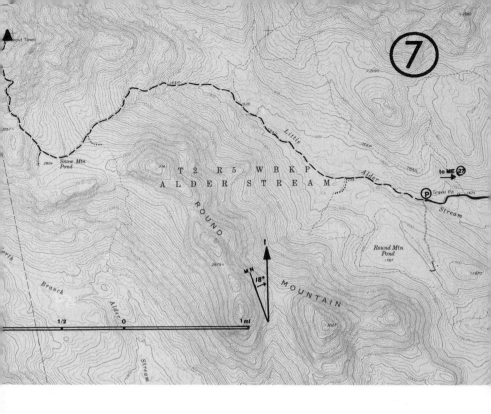

Old Speck   *Photo by Thomas R. Berrian*

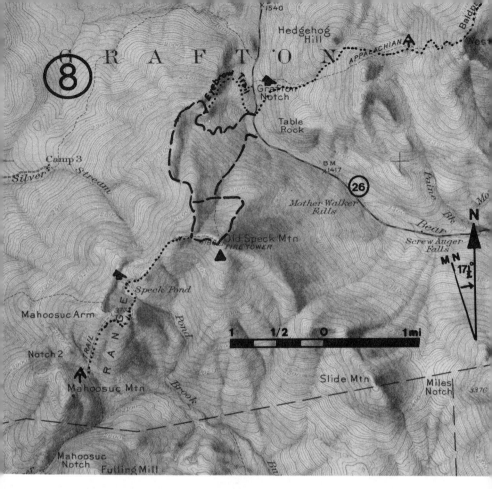

Additional Peaks of the New England Hundred Highest in Maine

Mountain	Elevation:ft/m	USGS Quad
Fort	3861/1177	Katahdin/Harrington Lake
Goose Eye	3860/1177	Old Speck
"Boundary Peak"	3845/1172	Little Kennebago Lake*
Bigelow, South Horn	3831/1168	Stratton
White Cap	3815/1163	Little Kennebago Lake*
Baldpate	3812/1162	Old Speck
Bigelow, North Horn	3810/1161	Stratton
East Kennebago	3791/1155	Quill Hill/Tim Mountain
Mahoosuc Arm	3790/1155	Old Speck
Elephant	3774/1150	Oquossoc
Abraham, Middle Peak	3765/1148	Phillips
Coe	3764/1147	Katahdin/Harrington La

*also use Canadian Woburn [21 E/7] quad. Canada Map Office, Surveys and Mapping Branch, Department of Energy, Mines and Resources, Ottawa, Ontario. CANADA K1A 0E9.

Chapter 3

The White Mountains of New Hampshire

The White Mountains, the highest mass of mountains in the Northeast, cover some 3,000 square miles in northern New Hampshire. Unlike the more uniform ridge line of the Green Mountains, New Hampshire's White Mountains rise in what at first appears to be a jumbled cluster. Most of these mountains, however, are part of ridges, though not very straight ones. Their origins are extremely complex; a chronological geological history would show several upliftings, and the results of folding, faulting and volcanic activity. A good portion of these mountains are made of igneous rocks, including granite (made from molten rock that formed deep within the earth). Other sections, including the mountains of the Presidential Range, are made of metamorphic rock (rocks that were transformed from one type to another by extreme heat and pressure). Both igneous and metamorphic rock resist erosion and it is this factor that accounts for their height relative to the valleys around them. According to most geologists, they stand as mountains because they have eroded more slowly than the land around them.

Glaciation shaped the White Mountains profoundly. The notches, including Franconia, Crawford and Pinkham, were rounded out by the advancing glacial ice sheet. Some ravines, like Tuckerman Ravine on the east face of Mt. Washington, are actually cirques, rounded out by smaller mountain glaciers both before and after the main ice sheet invaded the area. Numerous relics of the intense glaciation that the White Mountains received, including displaced boulders (erratics) and polished bedrock, can be found by the perceptive hiker.

The White Mountain region, which spreads out across northern New Hampshire in a roughly pear-shaped pattern, includes the following ranges:

Carter-Moriah Range: This 10-mile long range, with six peaks over 4,000 feet, lies east of the more imposing Presidential Range. On its southern end is the Wildcat Ski Area on Wildcat Mountain, on its northern is Mt. Moriah with its excellent views. Connecting most of these peaks is the 14-mile long Carter-Moriah Trail. The AMC Carter Notch Hut is located in rugged Carter Notch, in between Wildcat Mountain and Carter Dome.

Presidential Range: This range contains the highest summits in the Northeast, including massive Mt. Washington. Although it was not always the case, all the major peaks in this range are now named for U.S. presidents. Most of the area near the summits is above treeline, this being the largest alpine area in the United States east of the Rockies. In bad weather, and in any season, the danger to hikers in this exposed area should not be underestimated. The northern mountains, Madison, Adams and Jefferson, are rugged and require a 4,000-ft. or more elevation gain when climbed from the north. Mt. Washington has a road and cog railway to its summit and swarms with T-shirt clad, camera-carrying tourists during the summer. The southern Presidentials are more rounded but also extend into the alpine zone. The oldest continuously used mountain footpath in the country, the Crawford Path, begins in Crawford Notch and climbs to Mt. Washington by way of the southern Presidentials.

There are several summits in the Presidential Range, including Mt. Clay and Mt. Franklin, that rise above 4,000 feet but are not listed in this directory because they do not meet the requirements of any peakbagging list. The reason for this is that they fail to rise above their col (the gap, or pass, between peaks) with a nearby higher peak by a sufficient distance. In White Mountain climbing circles, this figure is 200 feet. (It doesn't matter that a peak doesn't rise 200' above the col with a lower peak).

Willey Range: Forming the western wall of glacially carved Crawford Notch, this small range includes three high summits. One of them, Mt. Field, is named for Darby Field, the first recorded European to climb Mt. Washington -- a mere 22 years after the arrival of the Pilgrims.

Sandwich Range: These mountains, located south of the Kancamagus Highway, were named for a succession of Indian chiefs including Passaconaway, Wonalancet, Kancamagus, Paugus, and Chocorua. Passaconaway, "Child of the Bear," lived during the early years of colonization in the 17th century, and was converted to Christianity by John Eliot in 1647. Wonalancet, his son, was a peaceful chief, but Kancamagus, his nephew, and Paugus were warriors who fought back against the English. Chocorua, for whom a particularly beautiful and dramatic peak is named, was said to have thrown himself off a cliff of this mountain after a misunderstanding concerning the death of his son.

Twin Range: In between the Willey Range and the Franconia Range, is a curved ridge line named for the double-peaked mountain at the end of the arc. From the cone of Garfield (also considered by some to be part of the Franconia Range) to the exposed ridges of Bondcliff, this range looks south over the vast Pemigewasset Wilderness.

Franconia Range: This range stands to the side of a great cleft in the mountains, rounded out by the passage of the glacial ice sheet. In this notch are a number of interesting geological features including the Flume gorge and the Old Man of the Mountains stone face on Profile Mountain. The range includes Mt. Lafayette and Mt. Lincoln both of which lie well above treeline. Garfield is often grouped with the Franconias.

Hiking Clubs in New Hampshire

Although founded in Boston, Massachusetts, the Appalachian Mountain Club (AMC) has long been involved with the White Mountains. The frequently updated AMC White Mountain Guide is the "bible" of the region and it comes with a set of maps for each section. The maps can be bought separately, printed either on fragile or more durable paper. The AMC has built and maintains a series of relatively isolated White Mountain huts that offer food and lodging. Access to these mountain hostels is by foot only and reservations are required. AMC also runs a shuttle bus that allows hikers to park at one spot and hike out to another. The AMC Pinkham Notch Camp, at the base of Mt. Washington, is open year-round and offers accommodations, a store stocking all their publications, and much more. If you hike the White Mountains, you will find that the AMC is ubiquitous. Many people think they, not the US Forest Service (who does), make the camping rules there.

There are a number of smaller hiking clubs based around the White Mountains, including the Randolph Mountain Club, the Wonalancet Out Door Club, the Chocorua Mountain Club and others. Many of these groups maintain trails and publish maps. Information on some of these is found in the last section of this book.

Land Ownership and Management

Nearly all of the 48 high peaks in New Hampshire lie within the White Mountain National Forest (WMNF). The exceptions are the summit of Mt. Washington, owned by the State of New Hampshire, and the summit of Mt. Moosilauke, owned by Dartmouth College. There are about 770,000 acres in New Hampshire and 47,000 acres in Maine that make up the forest. It is managed by the U.S. Forest Service for multiple uses, including recreation, timber production, watershed and wildlife protection. Only about 15% of the area falls within the full protection of the Wilderness Act of 1964 and thus may not be developed or logged. There are several USFS offices throughout the area.

In the past, the White Mountains were extensively logged. The parallel lines of forest seen on the slopes of the peaks are remnants of former logging roads. The Wilderness Trail through the Pemigewasset Valley is a former railroad bed used to carry out lumber from this remote area.

Trail Markings in the White Mountains

Due to heavy use, most White Mountain trails are easy to follow and they are well maintained. Some trails are unmarked except with signs at junctions with other trails. One exception is the Appalachian Trail which is marked with white blazes. The route of the AT coincides with many other trails (including the Twinway, Crawford Path and Carter-Moriah Trail) which, because they were built well before the arrival of the AT, retain their original names. Above treeline, trails are marked with paint on rocks or with cairns (rock piles). Some trails are marked with colored paint, frequently yellow. Side trails off the AT are usually marked with blue paint (the generally accepted standard for access trails to the AT).

photo by Chris Ryan

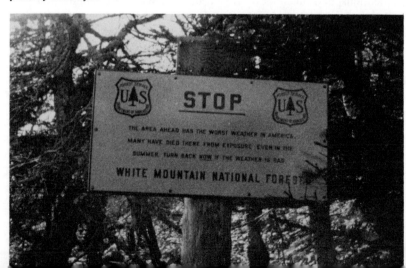

The White Mountains

Mountain	Elevation:ft/m	Date(s) Climbed
1. Washington	6288/1917	_____
2. Adams	5774/1760	_____
3. Jefferson	5712/1741	_____
4. Monroe	5384/1641*	_____
5. Madison	5367/1636	_____
6. Lafayette	5260/1603*	_____
7. Lincoln	5089/1551	_____
8. South Twin	4902/1494	_____
9. Carter Dome	4832/1473	_____
10. Moosilauke	4802/1464	_____
11. Eisenhower	4761/1451	_____
12. North Twin	4761/1451	_____
13. Bond	4698/1432	_____
14. Carrigain	4680/1426	_____
15. Middle Carter	4610/1405*	_____
16. West Bond	4540/1384*	_____
17. Garfield	4500/1372*	_____
18. Liberty	4459/1359	_____
19. South Carter	4430/1350*	_____
20. Wildcat	4422/1348	_____
21. Hancock	4403/1342	_____
22. South Kinsman	4358/1328	_____
23. Osceola	4340/1323*	_____
24. Flume	4328/1319	_____
25. Field	4326/1319	_____
26. Pierce (Clinton)	4310/1314	_____
27. Willey	4302/1311	_____
28. North Kinsman	4293/1309	_____
29. South Hancock	4274/1302	_____
30. Bondcliff	4265/1300	_____
31. Zealand	4260/1298*	_____
32. Cabot	4170/1271*	_____
33. East Osceola	4156/1267	_____
34. North Tripyramid	4140/1262	_____
35. Middle Tripyramid	4110/1253	_____
36. Cannon	4100/1250*	_____

37. Passaconaway	4060/1237	_____
38. Hale	4054/1236	_____
39. Jackson	4052/1235	_____
40. Moriah	4049/1234	_____
41. Tom	4047/1234	_____
42. Wildcat E	4041/1232	_____
43. Owl's Head	4025/1227	_____
44. Galehead	4024/1227	_____
45. Whiteface	4010/1222*	_____
46. Waumbek	4006/1221	_____
47. Isolation	4005/1221	_____
48. Tecumseh	4003/1220	_____

Elevations based on estimates from contour intervals. Source: AMC White Mountain Guide, 25th edition, 1992.

On Carter Dome   *Photo by Brett Gordon*

DIRECTORY OF HIGH SUMMITS IN THE WHITE MOUNTAINS

The Carter-Moriah Range

Moriah (9)

Elevation: 4,049 ft./1234 m.
USGS Quads/Coordinates: 7.5' Carter Dome, 7.5' Berlin, 7.5' Wild River: 44N20/71W08.
Best Maps: AMC #7 - Carter-Mahoosuc, Preston's Washington and Lafayette Trail Maps, DeLorme's Trail Map and Guide to the White Mountain National Forest.
Access: From US 2 near Gorham/NH 16 south of Gorham.
Trails to Summit: The Carter-Moriah Trail from near US 2 reaches the summit directly in 4.5 miles. The Stony Brook Trail from NH 16 leads to the Carter-Moriah Trail (AT), which leads to the summit in about 5 miles total. Other less direct options are the Moriah Brook Trail from Wild River Trail (and Campground) and the Rattle River Trail (AT) from US 2.
Comments: The exposed summit ledges of this mountain offer excellent views of the Carters, the Presidentials and the Mahoosucs.

Middle Carter (10)

Elevation: 4610 ft./1405 m.
USGS Quad/Coordinates: 7.5' Carter Dome: 44N18/71W10.
Best Maps: AMC #7 - Carter-Mahoosuc, Preston's Washington and Lafayette Trail Maps, DeLorme's Trail Map and Guide to the White Mountain National Forest.
Access: NH 16 about 2.5 miles north of Mt. Washington Auto Road.
Trails to Summit: Imp Trail to North Carter Trail to Carter- Moriah Trail (AT) (about 5 mi. to summit). It is also frequently climbed from Zeta Pass along with South Carter (see below).
Comments: The summit is wooded but has several overlooks, the best just north of the summit.

On the Carter-Moriah Trail   *Photo by Mark Feller*

South Carter (10)

Elevation: 4430 ft./1350 m.
USGS Quad/Coordinates: 7.5' Carter Dome: 44N17/71W11.
Best Maps: AMC #7 - Carter-Mahoosuc, Preston's Washington and Lafayette Trail Maps, DeLorme's Trail Map and Guide to the White Mountain National Forest.
Access: North of Pinkham Notch off NH 16.
Trails to Summit: The Carter-Moriah Trail (AT) crosses over the summit. Nearest access is via the Nineteen Mile Brook Trail to the Carter Dome Trail (about 4.6 mi. to summit).
Comments: The summit is wooded. Mt. Hight to the south and closer to Carter Dome, is a rocky exposed peak with good views.

Carter Dome (11)
See also (10)

Elevation: 4832 ft./1473 m.
USGS Quad/Coordinates: 7.5' Carter Dome: 44N16/71W11.
Best Maps: AMC #7 - Carter-Mahoosuc, Preston's Washington and Lafayette Trail Maps, DeLorme's Trail Map and Guide to the White Mountain National Forest. **Access:** North of Pinkham Notch of NH 16.

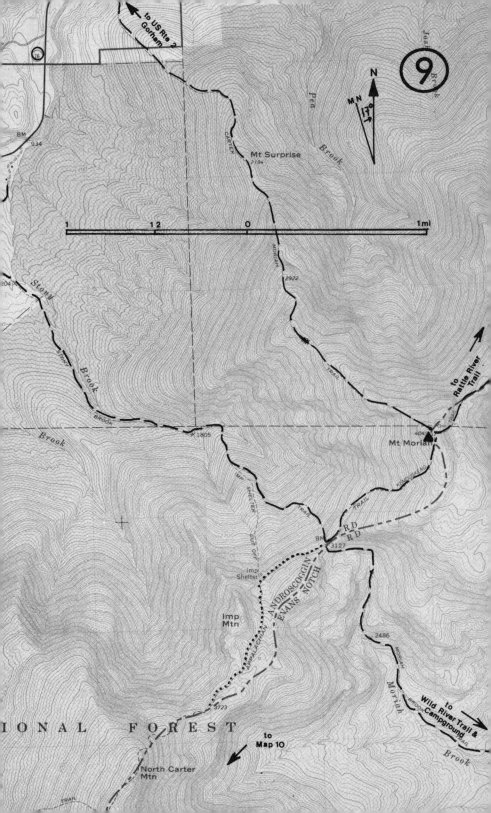

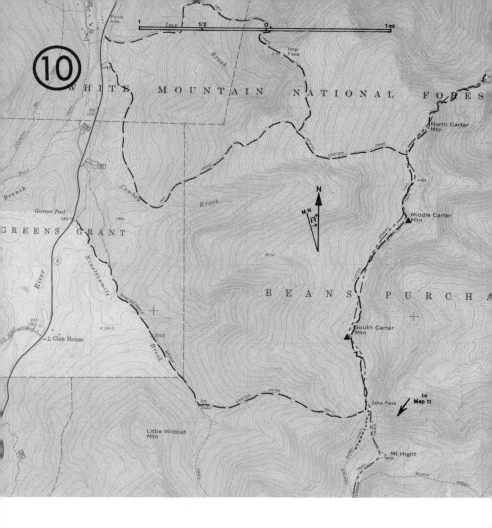

Trails to Summit: Options include (from the north) the Nineteen Mile Brook Trail or (from the south) the Wildcat River Trail to Carter Notch, then the Carter-Moriah Trail (AT) to the summit. The Rainbow Trail from the Wild River Trail in Perkins Notch ascends the mountain directly from the east. The Carter Dome Trail also reaches the summit from Zeta Pass to the north.

Comments: The flat summit, nearly above treeline, offers extensive views. This mountain stands opposite Wildcat Mountain with Carter Notch between them. In the notch is an AMC hut and two small lakes. To the north along the Carter-Moriah Trail (AT) is Mt. Hight which has a rocky summit.

Wildcat (11)

Elevation: 4422 ft./1348 m.

USGS Quads/Coordinates: 7.5' Carter Dome, 7.5' Jackson: 44N16/71W12.

Best Maps: AMC #7 - Carter-Mahoosuc, Preston's Washington and Lafayette Trail Maps, DeLorme's Trail Map and Guide to the White Mountain National Forest.

Access: Pinkham Notch (NH 16).

Trails to Summit: From Carter Notch the Wildcat Ridge Trail reaches the summit. Access to Carter Notch is via the Nineteen Mile Brook Trail (4.3 mi.). Another option is to reach Carter Notch from the south via the Bog Brook and Wildcat River trails (5 mi.).

Comments: Technically, this summit is Wildcat "A," the highest of the several alphabetical summits of the Wildcat Ridge, a mountain on which a ski area exists. The summit is wooded but there is an overlook down into Carter Notch 1,000 ft. below.

Wildcat "E" (11)

Elevation: 4041 ft./1232 m.

USGS Quads/Coordinates: 7.5' Carter Dome, 7.5' Jackson: 44N13/71W15.

Best Maps: AMC #6 - Mt. Washington Range, AMC #7 - Carter-Mahoosuc, Preston's Washington and Lafayette Trail Maps, DeLorme's Trail Map and Guide to the White Mountain National Forest.

Access: Pinkham Notch (NH 16), Glen Ellis Falls parking lot.

Trails to Summit: Wildcat Ridge Trail.

Comments: This is one of several summits on the wooded Wildcat Ridge, located above the Wildcat ski area. There are several overlooks on the way to the summit on the Wildcat Ridge Trail from Pinkham Notch, and a lookout tower to the east on top of nearby Wildcat "D." Recent maps show that Wildcat "D" is higher than "E" and it will eventually become the official 4000-footer summit.

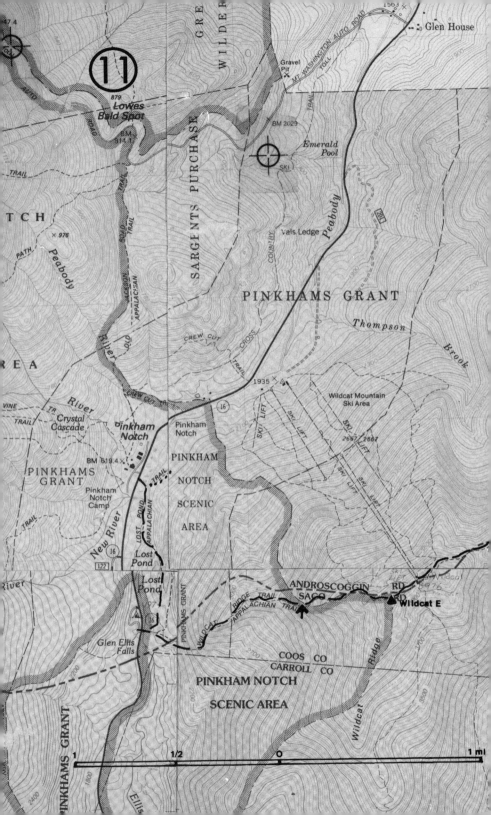

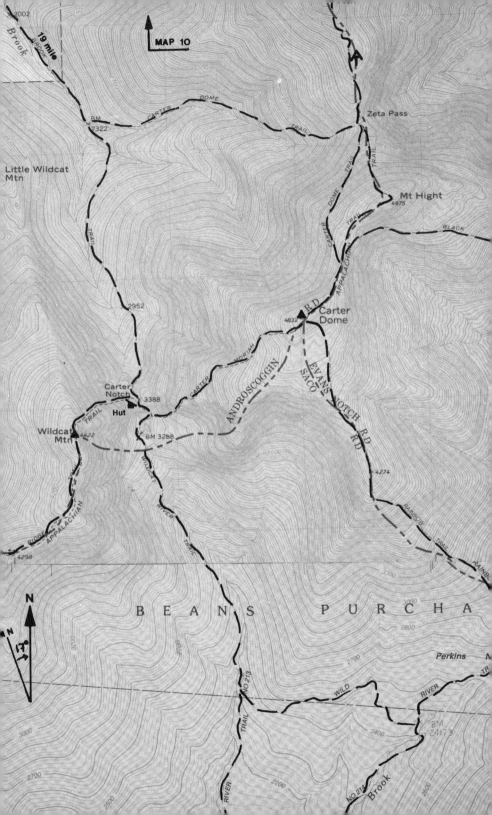

MAP 10

Brook

19 mile BROOK

BM
2322

CARTER DOME TRAIL

Zeta Pass

Little Wildcat
Mtn

TRAIL

Mt Hight
4675

BLACK

CARTER DOME TRAIL

2952

APPALACHIAN

R.D

Carter
Dome
4832

MORIAH

CARTER

Carter
Notch
3388

ANDROSCOGGIN

EVANS
SACO

NOTCH
R.D

Wildcat
Mtn
4422

TRAIL

Hut

BM 3288

3500

4274

WILDCAT

RIDGE

APPALACHIAN

RIVER

RAINBOW

TRAIL

TRAIL

4298

RAINBOW

5300

N

N

B E A N S   P U R C H A

3200

3000

2800

Perkins

RIVER

2700

TRAIL

NO 213

WILD

RIVER

BM
2417

3000

2400

2700

2500

RIVER

NO 21

Brook

2000

2600

Pilot and Pliny Ranges

Cabot (12)

Elevation: 4170 ft./1271 m. **USGS Quads/Coordinates:** 15' Percy, 15' Mt. Washington: 44N30/71W25.
Best Maps: AMC #8 - Pilot, Preston's Washington and Lafayette Trail Maps, DeLorme's Trail Map and Guide to the White Mountain National Forest.
Access: North of US 2. Complex directions - see AMC White Mountain Guide.
Trail to Summit: Mt. Cabot Trail (3.9 mi.).
Comments: The summit is wooded but a former fire tower site offers views. Bunnell Rock, en route to the summit, offers an excellent southward view.

Waumbek (12)

Elevation: 4006 ft./1221 m.
USGS Quads/Coordinates: 7.5' x 15' Pliny Range, 15' Mt. Washington: 44N26/71W25.
Best Maps: AMC #8 - Pilot, Preston's Washington and Lafayette Trail Maps, DeLorme's Trail Map and Guide to the White Mountain National Forest.
Access: From north of US 2.
Trail to Summit: Mt. Starr King Trail (3.6 mi.).
Comments: Mt. Waumbek is the highest summit in this small range. Though its summit is wooded, there are good views from the summit of Mt. Starr King over which the trail crosses. The Starr King Trail was named for Thomas Starr King, author of a popular 19th century book on the White Mountains.

The Presidential Range

Madison (13)

Elevation: 5363 ft./1636 m.
USGS Quads/Coordinates: 15' Mt. Washington, 7.5' Mt. Washington
S.E.: 44N20/71W17.
Best Maps: AMC #6 - Mt. Washington Range, Preston's Washington and
Lafayette Trail Maps, DeLorme's Trail Map and Guide to the White
Mountain National Forest.
Access: US 2, NH 16 (Dolly Copp Campground).
Trails to Summit: Many, including the strenuous Howker Ridge Trail
(4.5 mi.) and the dangerously exposed Watson Path route (4.1 mi.) from
the north. The safest routes are via the Osgood Trail from the Great Gulf
to the southeast, or the Valley Way Trail from north. The Daniel Webster
Scout Trail climbs from the east, connects with the Osgood Trail and
reaches the summit in 4.1 miles.
Comments: Mt. Madison is the northernmost major peak of the
Presidential Range and, like the others, rises well above treeline. From its
summit to the Peabody River, only 3 miles to the east, is a drop of 4,000
feet. Between this mountain and Mt. Adams to the southwest, lies the
AMC Madison Hut and the tiny Star Lake.

Adams (13)

Elevation: 5798 ft./1760 m.
USGS Quads/Coordinates: 15' Mt. Washington, 7.5' Mt. Washington
S.E.: 44N19/71W17.
Best Maps: AMC #6 - Mt. Washington Range, Preston's Washington and
Lafayette Trail Maps, DeLorme's Trail Map and Guide to the White
Mountain National Forest.
Access: From US 2 or NH 16 (Dolly Copp Campground).
Trails to Summit: Many, including Lowe's Path (4.8 mi.) and the Air
Line trail (4.3) from US 2 (Appalachia) to the north, and the Madison
Gulf Trail/Osgood Trail (5.7 mi.) from the southeast off the Mt.
Washington Auto Road.
Comments: Mt. Adams is the second highest summit in the Northeast. It's
summit is a rocky cone that tapers to a point and towers above everything
except Mt. Washington which dominates the horizon to the southeast over

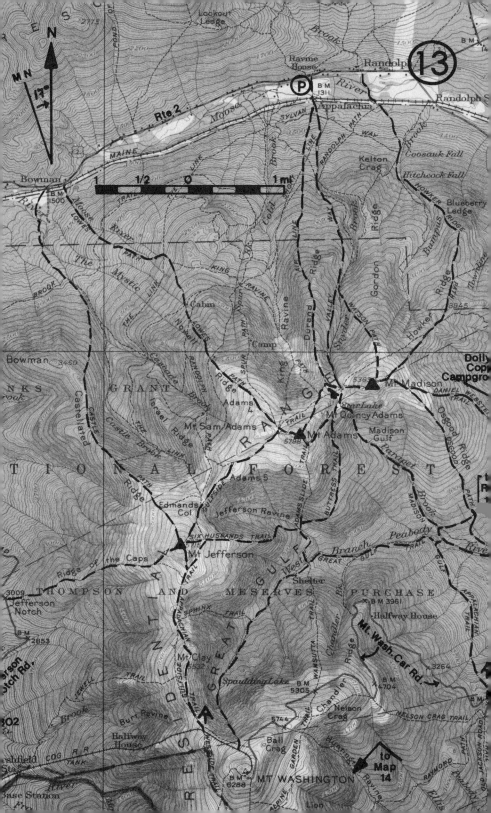

the Great Gulf. Two lesser summits are part of its mass; Mt. Sam Adams to the west and Mt. Quincy Adams to the north. A climb of the peak via the Air Line trail from the Appalachia parking area off US 2 requires an elevation gain of about 4,500 ft.

Jefferson (13)

Elevation: 5715 ft./1741 m.
USGS Quads/Coordinates: 15' Mt. Washington, 7.5' Mt. Washington S.E.: 44N18/71W19.
Best Maps: AMC #6 - Mt. Washington Range, Preston's Washington and Lafayette Trail Maps, DeLorme's Trail Map and Guide to the White Mountain National Forest.
Access: From US 2, Jefferson Notch Road, or NH 16.
Trails to Summit: Many, including the Caps Ridge Trail (2.5 mi.) from the west, the Castle Trail (5 mi.) from the north, and the Great Gulf/Six Husbands route (6.9 mi.) from the east.
Comments: Mt. Jefferson, like the other northern Presidential mountains (Adams, Madison and Clay) is well above treeline and offers excellent views from its three higher summits. Below the summit to the south is a broad alpine area called Monticello Lawn.

Star Lake between Madison and Adams

Washington (14)

Elevation: 6288 ft./1917 m.
USGS Quads/Coordinates: 15' Mt. Washington, 7.5' Mt. Washington
S.E.: 44N16/71W18.
Best Maps: AMC #6 - Mt. Washington Range, Preston's Washington and
Lafayette Trail Maps, DeLorme's Trail Map and Guide to the White
Mountain National Forest.
Access: From Pinkham Notch (NH 16) or from Crawford Notch (US 302).
Trails to Summit: Many trails ascend this huge mountain. The most
popular are the Tuckerman Ravine Trail (4.2 mi.) from the east, the
Ammonoosuc Ravine Trail to the Crawford Path (4.5 mi.) from the west,
and the Crawford Path itself (8.2 mi.) from the southwest. From the
northeast the Great Gulf Trail reaches the summit in 7.8 miles (the last .5
is via Gulfside Trail). A number of other routes are possible as are
combinations of several trails. You can also drive or take the cog railway
but it doesn't count as a climb.
Comments: Mt. Washington is the highest peak in the Northeast and
towers over the second, third, fourth and fifth highest summits of this
region located nearby. East of the Mississippi, only the highest summits of
the southern Appalachians are taller. Unlike the southern mountains,
however, Mt. Washington's summit lies well above treeline (which begins
between 4,000 and 5,000 ft. in the Northeast). As a result, the landscape
on this mountain and others nearby is devoid of trees and therefore
exposed to the elements. The conditions above treeline here are always
potentially dangerous and numerous deaths have occurred over the years.

Mt. Washington was first climbed in 1642, just over twenty years after
the Pilgrims landed, by Darby Field and his Native American guides.
Since then it has seen a long and varied human history, including trail and
hotel building, construction of a road and a railway up the mountain, and
the planting of a weather observatory on the summit. On the summit today
are a number of buildings that house weather instruments, TV
transmitters, a snack bar (try the chili), and a museum. The crowds in
summer, the inexperienced and weary hikers who didn't know what they
were getting themselves into, the cars and the whistle-blowing of the train,
all make Mt. Washington's summit a great destination for the
contemporary anthropologist, though not for the hiker seeking solitude.
Fortunately, the alpine area surrounding this mountain is so vast that
solitude and great beauty can be found not far away down one of the many
trails.

Mt. Washington from Mt. Adams

The geography of Mt. Washington and its surroundings is unlike anything else in New England. For miles to the north and south, high ridges above treeline are exposed to some of the worst weather in the world. In spite of this constant punishment from the weather, the area supports a community of alpine flowering plants, mosses, and lichens that normally grow in northern Canada. Mt. Washington's height is such that much of the time its cold and windy summit is covered by clouds. The mass of the mountain is so huge that it once supported several glaciers before and after previous ice ages. The effects of these glaciers produced Huntington and Tuckerman's Ravine on its eastern face, and the immense Great Gulf which lies to the north.

Monroe (14)

Elevation: 5385 ft./1641 m.
USGS Quads/Coordinates: 15' Mt. Washington, 7.5 Mt. Washington S.E.: 44N15/71W19.
Best Maps: AMC #6 - Mt. Washington Range, Preston's Washington and Lafayette Trail Maps, DeLorme's Trail Map and Guide to the White Mountain National Forest.
Access: From Crawford Notch (US 302) and Mt. Clinton Road, or from Pinkham Notch (NH 16).
Trail to Summit: Crawford Path via Mt. Monroe Loop (7 mi.), Ammonoosuc Ravine Trail to Mt. Monroe Loop (3.5 mi.).
Comments: Located to the southwest of Mt. Washington, this double-humped summit rises above an alpine plateau, a part of which is closed to

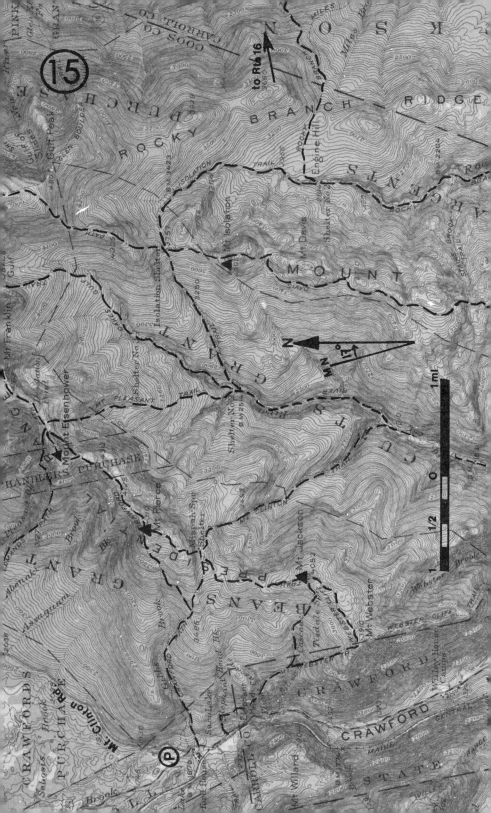

The southern slopes of Mt. Washington from Mt. Jackson

hikers to protect fragile and rare plant species. The summit is above treeline and offers a fine view over the Lakes of the Clouds, and the AMC hut of the same name, toward Mt. Washington. It is an easy climb from the hut via a portion of the Mt. Monroe Loop; many hikers staying there do it in less than a half hour.

Eisenhower (15)

Elevation: 4761 ft./1451 m.
USGS Quads/Coordinates: 15' Crawford Notch, 7.5' Stairs Mountain: 44N14/71W21.
Best Maps: AMC #6 - Mt. Washington Range, Preston's Washington and Lafayette Trail Maps, DeLorme's Trail Map and Guide to the White Mountain National Forest.
Access: From Crawford Notch (US 302) and Mt. Clinton Road.
Trails to Summit: The Edmands Path (3.4 mi.) and the Crawford Path (4.5 mi.) are the most direct routes to the summit. Both of these routes utilize the Eisenhower Loop which crosses over the summit parallel to the Crawford Path.
Comments: The summit of this mountain, crossed by the Mt. Eisenhower Loop, is a large, bare dome offering views in all directions. A large cairn marks the exact summit. It was formerly called Mt. Pleasant.

Pierce (Clinton) (15)

Elevation: 4312 ft./1314 m.
USGS Quads/Coordinates: 15' Crawford Notch, 7.5' Stairs Mountain: 44N13/71W22.
Best Maps: AMC #6 - Mt. Washington Range, Preston's Washington and Lafayette Trail Maps, DeLorme's Trail Map and Guide to the White Mountain National Forest.
Access: From Crawford Notch (US 302).
Trails to Summit: Crawford Path (3 mi.), Webster Cliff Trail (7.4 mi.).
Comments: This mountain was officially named Mt. Pierce in 1913, after the New Hampshire-born president, but was originally named Mt. Clinton. The summit is just missed by the Crawford Path, which runs from Crawford Notch to the summit of Mt. Washington. The trail that leads to

the partially wooded summit is the end of the Webster Cliff Trail. The flat and broad summit offers good views to the west, north and east. The summit is located about a mile from the AMC Mizpah Hut.

Jackson (15)

Elevation: 4052 ft./1235 m.
USGS Quads/Coordinates: 15' Crawford Notch, 7.5' Crawford Notch: 44N12/71W23.
Best Maps: AMC #6 - Mt. Washington Range, Preston's Washington and Lafayette Trail Maps, DeLorme's Trail Map and Guide to the White Mountain National Forest.
Access: Crawford Notch (US 302).
Trails to Summit: Webster-Jackson Trail (2.6 mi.), Webster Cliff Trail (4.7 mi.).
Comments: This mountain was not named for president Andrew Jackson, but for Charles Jackson, a New Hampshire State Geologist. Its open summit is reached most easily from Crawford Notch via the Webster-Jackson Trail. The partially bare summit offers a dramatic view of Mt. Washington and the southern peaks. The summit is 1.7 miles from the AMC Mizpah Hut.

Isolation (15)

Elevation: 4005 ft./1221 m.
USGS Quads/Coordinates: 15' Crawford Notch, 7.5' Stairs Mountain: 44N13/71W18.
Best Maps: AMC #6 - Mt. Washington Range, Preston's Washington and Lafayette Trail Maps, DeLorme's Trail Map and Guide to the White Mountain National Forest.
Access: South of Pinkham Notch (NH 16); south of Crawford Notch (US 302).
Trails to Summit: Rocky Branch Trail to Isolation Trail (7.3 mi.), Davis Path (9.7 mi.).
Comments: Mt. Isolation is a remote open summit located along one of the early bridle paths leading to Mt. Washington constructed by Nathaniel P.T. Davis in 1844. The most direct route to this summit is via the north end of the Rocky Branch Trail from NH 16. Another alternative is to follow the Davis Path from US 302 for about 9.7 miles.

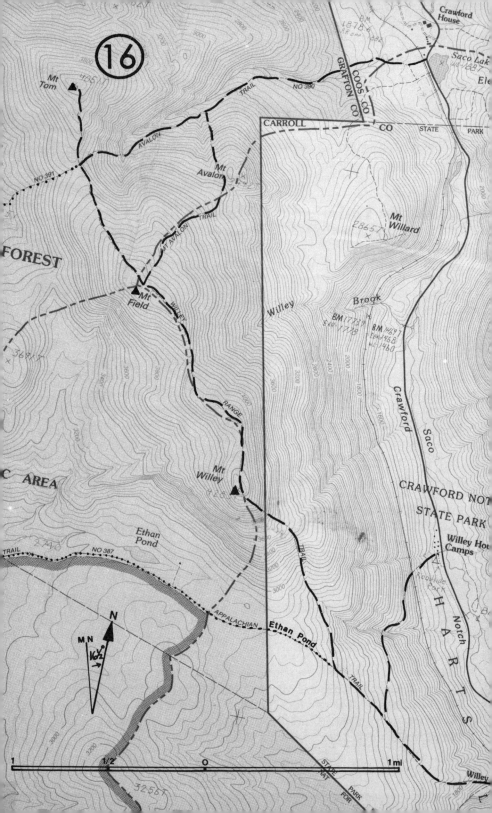

Central White Mountains

Tom (16)

Elevation: 4047 ft./1234 m.
USGS Quad/Coordinates: 7.5' Crawford Notch: 44N13/71W27.
Best Maps: AMC #5 - Franconia, Preston's Washington and Lafayette Trail Maps, DeLorme's Trail Map and Guide to the White Mountain National Forest.
Access: Crawford Notch (US 302).
Trails to Summit: The Avalon Trial from Crawford Depot (US 302) reaches the A-Z Trail which then crosses the Willey Range Trail in the col between Mt. Tom and Mt. Field; a spur trail heads north to the summit (total distance is 2.9 mi.).
Comments: Mt. Tom is the northernmost peak in the Willey Range, the ridge that forms the western wall of Crawford Notch. This wooded peak was named for Thomas Crawford, a member of the Crawford family. During the early 19th century, the Crawfords offered tourists lodging and guided excursions to the White Mountain summits.

Field (16)

Elevation: 4326 ft./1319 m.
USGS Quad/Coordinates: 7.5' Crawford Notch: 44N12/71W26.
Best Maps: AMC #5 - Franconia, Preston's Washington and Lafayette Trail Maps, DeLorme's Trail Map and Guide to the White Mountain National Forest.
Access: Crawford Notch (US 302).
Trails to Summit: Avalon Trail to Willey Range Trail (2.8 mi.).
Comments: The middle summit in the Willey Range, Mt. Field was named for Darby Field, the first colonist to climb Mt. Washington. An approach via the Avalon Trail offers the best views en route. Nearby Mt. Avalon offers good views.

Willey (16)

Elevation: 4302 ft./1311 m.
USGS Quad/Coordinates: 7.5' Crawford Notch: 44N11/71W25.
Best Maps: AMC #5 - Franconia, Preston's Washington and Lafayette

Trail Maps, DeLorme's Trail Map and Guide to the White Mountain National Forest.

Access: Crawford Notch (US 302).

Trail to Summit: Ethan Pond Trail from Willey House Station (US 302) to Willey Range Trail (2.7 mi.).

Comments: This mountain was named after the Willey family, who lived below it and were killed by a landslide in 1826. Summit views are from an unmarked path heading east just before the summit and from a southern overlook on the main trail.

Carrigain (17)

Elevation: 4680 ft./1426 m.

USGS Quad/Coordinates: 7.5' Mt. Carrigain: 44N06/71W27.

Best Maps: AMC #5 - Franconia, Preston's Washington and Lafayette Trail Maps, DeLorme's Trail Map and Guide to the White Mountain National Forest.

Access: Crawford Notch (US 302) via Sawyer River Road.

Trail to Summit: Signal Ridge Trail (5 mi.).

Comments: This mountain, located near the exact center of the White Mountains, has a wooded summit with an observation platform offering 360-degree views. Signal Ridge, a long southeastern extension of the mountain, is exposed and offers excellent views in all directions. Mt. Carrigain was named for a 19th century New Hampshire secretary of state who also did some cartographic work in the region. The Desolation Trail, which begins deep in the Pemigewasset Wilderness, climbs the mountain from the north . A loop hike is possible utilizing it, the Signal Ridge Trail and the Carrigain Notch Trail.

Hancock, North Peak (18)
See also Map 20

Elevation: 4403 ft./1342 m.

USGS Quad/Coordinates: 7.5' Mt. Carrigain: 44N05/71W30.

Best Maps: AMC #5 - Franconia, Preston's Washington and Lafayette Trail Maps, DeLorme's Trail Map and Guide to the White Mountain National Forest.

Access: Kancamagus Highway.

Trails to Summit: Hancock Notch Trail to Cedar Brook Trail to Hancock

Signal Ridge from Carrigain

Loop Trail (4.3 mi.).
Comments: The elevation given above is that for the highest point on a long wooded ridge with several summits. There is an overlook looking south near the summit. The Hancock Loop Trail crosses both Hancock summits.

South Hancock (18)
See also Map 20

Elevation: 4274 ft./1303 m.
USGS Quad/Coordinates: 7.5' Mt. Carrigain: 44N04/71W29.
Best Maps: AMC #5 - Franconia, Preston's Washington and Lafayette Trail Maps, DeLorme's Trail Map and Guide to the White Mountain National Forest.
Access: Kancamagus Highway.
Trails to Summit: Hancock Notch Trail to Cedar Brook Trail to Hancock Loop Trail (4.1 mi.).
Comments: The wooded southern summit of the Hancock ridge has an overlook with a vista to the east.

Sandwich Range

Passaconaway (19)

Elevation: 4060 ft./1237 m.
USGS Quads/Coordinates: 15' Mt. Chocorua, 7.5 Mt. Tripyramid: 43N57/71W23.
Best Maps: AMC #4 - Chocorua-Waterville Map, Preston's Washington and Lafayette Trail Maps, DeLorme's Trail Map and Guide to the White Mountain National Forest, Wonalancet Out Door Club Sandwich Range Wilderness Map.
Access: Kancamagus Highway. Ferncroft Road off NH 113A at Wonalancet Village.
Trails to Summit: Northern approach from Kancamagus Highway: Olivarian Brook to Passaconaway Cutoff to Square Ledge to Walden trails (5.1 mi.). Southern approach from Ferncroft Road via Dicey's Mill Trail (4.6 mi.).
Comments: This mountain was named for a legendary Indian chief who lived during the early colonial times. The summit is wooded but there are

overlooks to the east and north. Between and southeast of Passaconaway and Whiteface is the Bowl, an isolated natural area that is located within the Sandwich Range Wilderness. A number of other routes to the summit are possible, given the large number of trails in the area.

Whiteface (19)

Elevation: 4015 ft./1222 m.
USGS Quads/Coordinates: 15' Mt. Chocorua, 7.5' Mt. Tripyramid: 43N56/71W25.
Best Maps: AMC #4 - Chocorua-Waterville Map, Preston's Washington and Lafayette Trail Maps, DeLorme's Trail Map and Guide to the White Mountain National Forest, Wonalancet Out Door Club Sandwich Range Wilderness Map.
Access: Ferncroft Road off NH 113A at Wonalancet Village or Whiteface Intervale Road. Kancamagus Highway.
Trails to Summit: From Ferncroft Road: Blueberry Ledge Trail to Rollins/Downes Brook trails (3.9 mi.). From Whiteface Intervale Road: Flat Mountain Pond Trail/McCrillis Trail to Rollins/Downes Brook trails (5.2 mi.). From Kancamagus Highway: Downes Brook Trail (6.4 mi.).
Comments: Although the actual summit of this mountain is wooded, the lower south summit is exposed and offers excellent views over steep ledges. The junction of the Blueberry Ledge, McCrillis and Downes Brook trails is located near these ledges.

Tripyramid from Osceola

Tripyramid, North Peak (19)

Elevation: 4140 ft./1262 m.
USGS Quads/Coordinates: 15' Mt. Chocorua, 7.5' Mt. Tripyramid: 43N58/71W27.
Best Maps: AMC #4 - Chocorua-Waterville Map, Preston's Washington and Lafayette Trail Maps, DeLorme's Trail Map and Guide to the White Mountain National Forest, Wonalancet Out Door Club Sandwich Range Wilderness Map.
Access: Waterville Valley. Kancamagus Highway.
Trails to Summit: From Waterville Valley: Livermore Trail to Mt. Tripyramid Trail (3.8 mi.). From Kancamagus Highway: Pine Bend Brook Trail (4 mi.), Sabbaday Brook Trail to Mt. Tripyramid Trail (5.4 mi.).
Comments: This striking mountain was named for the three pyramid-shaped peaks that top a narrow ridge. There are excellent views to the west and north from the top of a slide on this mountain.

Tripyramid, Middle Peak (19)

Elevation: 4110 ft./1253 m.
USGS Quads/Coordinates: 15' Mt. Chocorua, 7.5' Mt. Tripyramid: 43N57/71W27.
Best Maps: AMC #4 - Chocorua-Waterville Map, Preston's Washington and Lafayette Trail Maps, DeLorme's Trail Map and Guide to the White Mountain National Forest, Wonalancet Out Door Club Sandwich Range Wilderness Map.
Access: Waterville Valley. Kancamagus Highway.
Trails to Summit: From Waterville Valley: Livermore Trail to Mt. Tripyramid Trail (4.6 mi.). From Kancamagus Highway: Pine Bend Brook Trail to Mt. Tripyramid Trail (4.8 mi.), Sabbaday Brook Trail to Mt. Tripyramid Trail (5.2 mi.).
Comments: There are good views from this summit and just below it to the east and west.

Sandwich (19)

Elevation: 3993 ft./1217 m.
USGS Quads/Coordinates: 7.5' Waterville Valley, 7.5' Mt. Tripyramid, 15' Mt. Chocorua: 43N54/71W30.

IVERMORE
Thornton Gap
19
West Branch
Brook
1648
River
Mad
Kancamagus
Flume Peak
The Flume
Flume
The Scaur
Livermore
2159
Brook
NTAIN
Mt Tecumseh
4004
Tecumseh
Brook
1623
Avalanche
Norway Rapids
Slide
The Ledges
Cascades
Cascade
Brook
BM 1519
Waterville Valley
Hardy
Snows Brook
Snows
WA
Mountain
Green Mtn
1510
TERVILLE
Snows
Brook
Mtn
Drakes
Bk
Waterville Forest Camp
1332
Shell Cascade
Sandwich
Fletcher Cascades
NAL
Mtn
Drakes
Brook
Flat Mou
Rte 49
BM 1179
Noon Peak
2870
Jennings Pk
3500
Ridge
Trail
Bald Knob
2318
Acteon
Sachem Peak
Sandwich Mtn
Sandwich Mtn
3993
Smarts Brook Trail
Sandwich Mtn Trail
GRAFTON CO
CARROLL CO
Algonquin Trail
Gleason Trail
Brook
TRAIL
RESTT
BROOK
Algonquin
Black Mtn
2626
to Sandwich Notch Rd
Black Mtn Pond
NGE
RA
WHITE MOUN
Atwood Pond

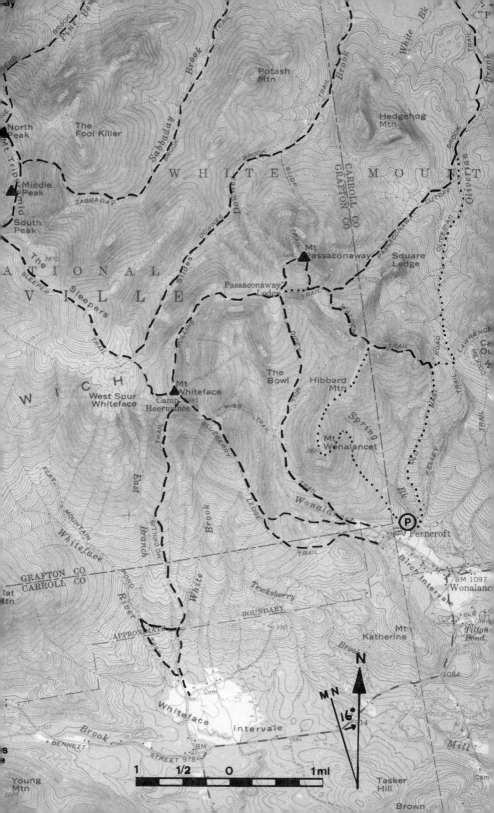

Best Maps: AMC #4 - Chocorua-Waterville Map, Preston's Washington and Lafayette Trail Maps, DeLorme's Trail Map and Guide to the White Mountain National Forest, Wonalancet Out Door Club Sandwich Range Wilderness Map.

Access: NH 49, Sandwich Notch Road, Bennett Street.

Trails to Summit: From NH 49: Sandwich Mountain Trail (3.9 mi.), Smarts Brook Trail to Sandwich Mountain Trail (5.7 mi.). From Sandwich Notch Road: Algonquin Trail (4.5 mi.). From Bennett Street at Jose's Bridge: Bennett Street Trail (4 mi.).

Comments: Sandwich Mountain, the most southerly of the high peaks of the White Mountains, is also called Sandwich Dome. It was formerly known as Black Mtn., this name having been retained for a southwestern spur. The Sandwich Mtn. Trail, including its side trail to Jennings Peak, offers good views in several place. The summit of Sandwich is partially wooded but offers a few views through the trees. The Algonquin Trail, which climbs the Black Mtn. ridge, offers excellent views from its ledges before reaching the summit of Sandwich.

Osceola, East Peak (20)

Elevation: 4156 ft./1267 m.

USGS Quads/Coordinates: 7.5' Mt. Osceola, 7.5' Waterville Valley: 44N00/71W31.

Best Maps: AMC #4 - Chocorua-Waterville Map, Preston's Washington and Lafayette Trail Maps, DeLorme's Trail Map and Guide to the White Mountain National Forest.

Access: From Tripoli Road/Waterville Valley or from Kancamagus Highway.

Trails to Summit: From Tripoli Road: Mount Osceola Trail (4.2 mi.), Greeley Ponds Trail to Mount Osceola Trail (5 mi.). From Kancamagus Highway: Greeley Ponds Trail to Mount Osceola Trail (2.8 mi.).

Comments: This peak is just to the northeast of Osceola, the main peak. The climb from the north (Kancamagus Highway) via Greeley Ponds Trail is particularly steep. The summit is wooded but there is a good vista to the northeast on the way up.

Osceola (20)

Elevation: 4340 ft./1323 m.

USGS Quads/Coordinates: 7.5' Mt. Osceola, 7.5' Waterville Valley: 44N00/71W32.

Best Maps: AMC #4 - Chocorua-Waterville Map, Preston's Washington and Lafayette Trail Maps, DeLorme's Trail Map and Guide to the White Mountain National Forest.

Access: Tripoli Road/Waterville Valley or from Kancamagus Highway.

Trails to Summit: From Tripoli Road: Mount Osceola Trail (3.2 mi.). From Kancamagus Highway: Greeley Ponds Trail to Mount Osceola Trail (3.8 mi.).

Comments: This peak, the highest in the Sandwich Range, was named for the chief of the Seminole people of Florida. The summit of Osceola is partially exposed and offers good views to East Peak, Tripyramid and the Waterville Valley. The concrete foundations of two fire towers still stand on the plaza-like slabs of the summit. Osceola is most easily reached from Tripoli Road. If the northern route is taken, Osceola, East Peak must be climbed on the way. Near the col between the two is one very steep section.

Tecumseh (20)

Elevation: 4003/1220 m.

USGS Quad/Coordinates: 7.5' Waterville Valley: 43N58/71W33.

Best Maps: AMC #4 - Chocorua-Waterville Map, Preston's Washington and Lafayette Trail Maps, DeLorme's Trail Map and Guide to the White Mountain National Forest.

Access: Waterville Valley/Tecumseh Ski Area. Tripoli Road.

Trail to Summit: Mt. Tecumseh Trail from ski area (2.2 mi.; relocations in process) or from Tripoli Road (3.1 mi.).

Comments: Named for a Shawnee chief, this mountain offers views toward Tripyramid in the east and Osceloa north. A ski operation exists on its slopes but its wooded summit, with some views, is interesting. The Sosman Trail from the summit heads south to the top of the ski lifts; a knob called White (or White's Peak) by the ski area. The Mt. Tecumseh Trail crosses over West Tecumseh, once listed as one of the New England hundred highest peaks, and then on to Tripoli Road. Portions of ski trails may be used to approach or descend from this summit.

The Twin Ranges

Hale (21)
See also Map 22

Elevation: 4054 ft./1236 m.
USGS Quad/Coordinates: 7.5' South Twin Mtn.: 44N13/71W31.
Best Maps: AMC #5 - Franconia, Preston's Washington and Lafayette Trail Maps, DeLorme's Trail Map and Guide to the White Mountain National Forest.
Access: Zealand Road off US 302.
Trails to Summit: Hale Brook Trail (2.2 mi.).
Comments: This mountain was named for Reverend Edward Everett Hale, author of "The Man Without a Country." The Hale Brook Trail is a relatively easy climb to the bare summit which offers good views, particularly to the south over Zealand Notch to Carrigain. A loop hike of about 9 mi. over the mountain and past the AMC Zealand Falls Hut is possible using the Hale Brook Trail/Lend a Hand Trail and Zealand Trail.

North Twin (22)

Elevation: 4761 ft./1451 m.
USGS Quad/Coordinates: 7.5' South Twin Mtn.: 44N12/71W33.
Best Maps: AMC #5 - Franconia, Preston's Washington and Lafayette Trail Maps, DeLorme's Trail Map and Guide to the White Mountain National Forest.
Access: From Haystack Road off US 3 or from the Twinway (AT) Trail connecting Galehead and Zealand AMC huts.
Trails to Summit: North Twin Trail (4.3 mi.), North Twin Spur (1.3 mi.).
Comments: Summit is wooded but a ledge facing west offers a particularly dramatic view of the Garfield Ridge and the Franconias with Galehead Hut in the foreground. South Twin is accessible from this summit via the 1.3 mile long North Twin Spur.

South Twin (22)

Elevation: 4902 ft./1494 m.
USGS Quad/Coordinates: 7.5' South Twin Mtn.: 44N11/71W33.

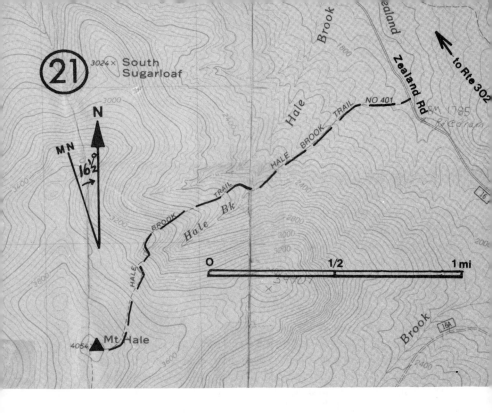

Best Maps: AMC #5 - Franconia, Preston's Washington and Lafayette Trail Maps, DeLorme's Trail Map and Guide to the White Mountain National Forest.

Access: From Gale River Loop Road (Fire Road 92/25) or Haystack Road both off US 3.

Trails to Summit: Gale River Trail to Garfield Ridge Trail to Twinway (5.4 mi.). North Twin Trail to North Twin Spur (5.6 mi.).

Comments: South Twin, one of the higher peaks in the area, has a small, rocky, but open summit with a wide panorama of the White Mountains. The summit of North Twin is located about 1 mile north and is reached via the North Twin Spur from South Twin's summit. The climb from Galehead Hut is quite steep, a beeline to the summit that gradually emerges at treeline just below the summit. The Garfield Ridge Trail and the Twinway are part of the Appalachian Trail (AT).

Galehead (22)

Elevation: 4024 ft./1227 m.
USGS Quad/Coordinates: 7.5' South Twin Mtn.: 44N11/71W34.
Best Maps: AMC #5 - Franconia, Preston's Washington and Lafayette

South Twin summit

Trail Maps, DeLorme's Trail Map and Guide to the White Mountain National Forest.

Access: From Gale River Loop Road (Fire Road 92) off US 3 via AMC Galehead hut.

Trails to Summit: Frost Trail from Galehead hut (.5 mi.). Access to hut is via Gale River to Garfield Ridge to Twinway trails.

Comments: Galehead, while dwarfed by its neighbor South Twin, is interesting in that it displays the classic shape of a mountain that has been severely glaciated. Its north face has been planed smooth while its south face drops abruptly. This feature is evident from Galehead Hut where the Frost Trail begins the easy climb to its wooded summit with limited views.

Zealand (22)

Elevation: 4301 ft./1298 m.

USGS Quad/Coordinates: 7.5' South Twin Mtn.: 44N10/71W31.

Best Maps: AMC #5 - Franconia, Preston's Washington and Lafayette Trail Maps, DeLorme's Trail Map and Guide to the White Mountain National Forest.

Access: Zealand Road off US 302.

Trails to Summit: Zealand Trail to Twinway (6 mi.). Note: the actual summit is 0.1 mi. north on a side path.

Comments: Zealand Mountain has a wooded summit. The Zealand Trail leads to the AMC Zealand Falls hut and connects to the Twinway (AT). There are excellent views from the Zeacliff outlook along the Twinway. The mountain and the other features in the area derive their names from the original name for the area, the New Zealand Valley.

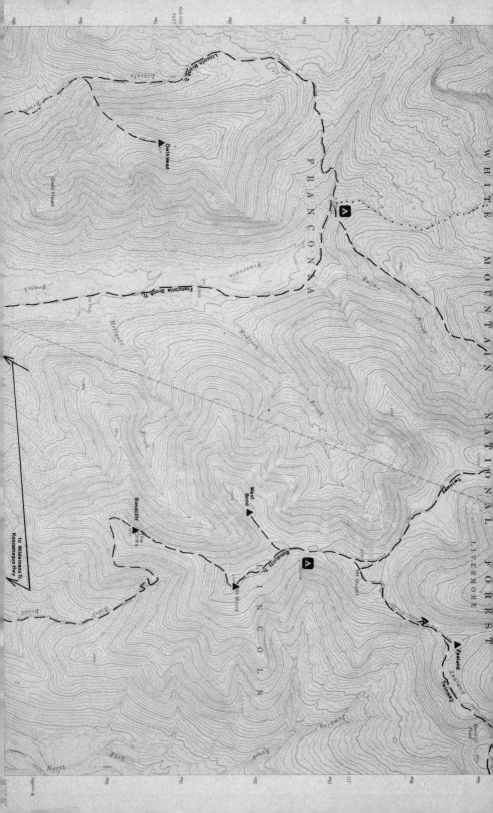

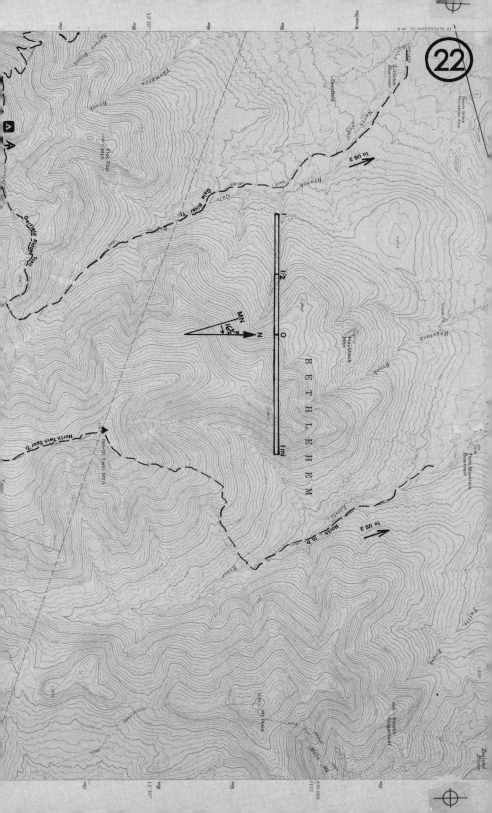

The cliffs on the western face of Bondcliff

Bond (22)

Elevation: 4698 ft./1432 m.
USGS Quad/Coordinates: 7.5' South Twin Mtn.: 44N09/71W32.
Best Maps: AMC #5 - Franconia, Preston's Washington and Lafayette Trail Maps, DeLorme's Trail Map and Guide to the White Mountain National Forest.
Access: The Bonds are not easily reached. Options include hiking south from US 302 via Zealand Trail and Twinway or north from the Kancamagus Highway via the Wilderness Trail. Another option is to utilize the AMC Galehead Hut; a 2-night stay with a day- hike to the Bonds.
Trails to Summit: Bondcliff Trail from Twinway (1.3 mi.), from Wilderness Trail (5.6 mi.). Total hiking distance from Zealand Road is 8.5 mi., from Kancamagus Highway is 10.3 mi.
Comments: This bare summit is part of a long north/south ridge with several peaks that overlooks the Pemigewasset River valley. The 360 degree views from this central and remote part of the White Mountains are expansive.

West Bond (22)

Elevation: 4526 ft./1384 m.
USGS Quad/Coordinates: 7.5' South Twin Mtn.: 44N09/71W33.
Best Maps: AMC #5 - Franconia, Preston's Washington and Lafayette Trail Maps, DeLorme's Trail Map and Guide to the White Mountain National Forest.
Access: See Mt. Bond.
Trails to Summit: West Bond Spur from Bondcliff Trail (0.5 mi.).
Comments: This rocky peak, a western extension of the Bond ridge, is perched above the vast Pemigewasset Wilderness due west of Mt. Bond. The view out to Bondcliff is particularly striking.

Bondcliff (22)

Elevation: 4265 ft./1300 m.
USGS Quad/Coordinates: 7.5' South Twin Mtn.: 44N08/71W33.

Best Maps: AMC #5 - Franconia, Preston's Washington and Lafayette Trail Maps, DeLorme's Trail Map and Guide to the White Mountain National Forest.
Access: See Mt. Bond
Trails to Summit: Bondcliff Trail: 4.4 mi. from Wilderness Trail, 2.5 mi. from the Twinway.
Comments: The long bare alpine summit and cliffs of this mountain make for some spectacular, though exposed, hiking. Because it is somewhat lower than the peaks around it, the views are quite spectacular. The cliffs on the western side of peak are steep and care should be take to stay away from them during bad weather.

Garfield (22)

Elevation: 4500 ft./1372 m.
USGS Quad/Coordinates: 7.5' South Twin Mtn.: 44N11/71W36.
Best Maps: AMC #5 - Franconia, Preston's Washington and Lafayette Trail Maps, DeLorme's Trail Map and Guide to the White Mountain National Forest.
Access: From US 3, Five Corners/Gale River Loop (Fire Road 92), or from Greenleaf or Galehead AMC huts.
Trails to Summit: Garfield Trail (5 mi.), Garfield Ridge Trail (3.1 mi. from AMC Galehead hut, 3.5 mi. from Mt. Lafayette summit). A loop hike is possible using the Garfield, Garfield Ridge and Gale River trails (11.5 mi.).
Comments: Mt. Garfield has a steep rocky cone that offers excellent views over the Pemigewasset Wilderness, the huge mass of Owl's Head mountain low in the foreground. It is located on a rugged, long and curving ridge that connects the Franconia Range with the Twin Range.

Owl's Head (22)

Elevation: 4025 ft./1227 m.
USGS Quad/Coordinates: 7.5' South Twin Mtn.: 44N08/71W36.
Best Maps: AMC #5 - Franconia, Preston's Washington and Lafayette Trail Maps, DeLorme's Trail Map and Guide to the White Mountain National Forest.
Access: Kancamagus Highway via Wilderness Trail. Another option is to descend from Galehead hut (requires a 2-night stay).

Trails to Summit: Wilderness to Franconia Brook to Lincoln Brook trails to Owl's Head Path (9 mi.).

Comments: This is a very remote mountain, in some ways the "Couchsachraga (see the Adirondacks) of the White Mountains." It's a long hike in, about 8 miles from the Kancamagus Highway via the Wilderness Trail, and another mile to its wooded summit. The trail ascends a slide from which there are some views to the Franconia Range. The slide is rough, loose and potentially dangerous. Cairns mark the route which is easier on the south side of the slide. A herd path leads to the actual summit.

Franconia Range

Lafayette (23)

Elevation: 5242 ft./1603 m.
USGS Quad/Coordinates: 7.5' Franconia: 44N10/71W39.
Best Maps: AMC #5 - Franconia, Preston's Washington and Lafayette Trail Maps, DeLorme's Trail Map and Guide to the White Mountain National Forest.
Access: From Franconia Notch Parkway (I-93).
Trails to Summit: Greenleaf Trail (3.8 mi.), Old Bridle Path to Greenleaf Trail (4 mi.), Skookumchuck Trail to Garfield Ridge Trail (5 mi.).
Comments: Originally called "Great Haystack," this peak was renamed for the Marquis de Lafayette. It is the northernmost peak of a high, narrow ridge that runs well above treeline and extends to Little Haystack Mountain. The views to the west over the Pemigewasset and the view to the east over Franconia Notch are excellent. Caution: this summit and ridge is exposed and can be extremely dangerous in bad weather. Below and west of the summit is the Greenleaf AMC Hut. The Franconia Ridge Trail runs for five miles along the high ridge between Lafayette and Mt. Flume.

Lincoln (23)

Elevation: 5089 ft./1551 m.
USGS Quad/Coordinates: 7.5' Franconia: 44N09/71W39.
Best Maps: AMC #5 - Franconia, Preston's Washington and Lafayette Trail Maps, DeLorme's Trail Map and Guide to the White Mountain

Top: Lincoln Mountain
Bottom: The summit of Mt. Flume

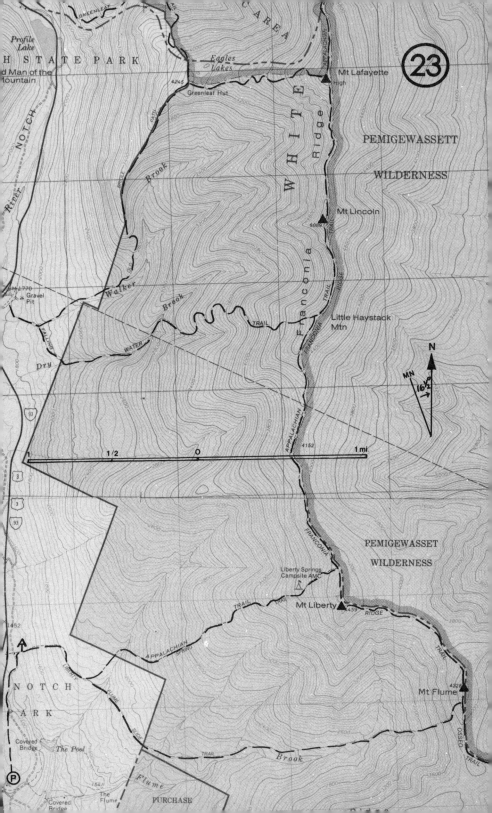

National Forest.

Access: From Franconia Notch Parkway (I-93).

Trails to Summit: Falling Waters Trail (3.9 mi.). Old Bridle Path to Franconia Ridge Trail (5 mi.).

Comments: Mt. Lincoln is located just north of a 2-mile long stretch of narrow, knife-edged ridge that is above treeline connecting Lincoln and Little Haystack Mountain. Conditions can be dangerous in bad weather due to such extreme exposure. A loop hike utilizing the Falling Waters, Franconia Ridge and Old Bridle Path passes over the summit of both Lincoln and Lafayette mountains (8.9 mi.).

Liberty (23)

Elevation: 4459 ft./1359 m.

USGS Quad/Coordinates: 7.5' Lincoln: 44N07/71W39.

Best Maps: AMC #5 - Franconia, Preston's Washington and Lafayette Trail Maps, DeLorme's Trail Map and Guide to the White Mountain National Forest.

Access: From Franconia Notch Parkway (I-93).

Trails to Summit: Liberty Spring Trail to Franconia Ridge Trail (3.2 mi.).

Comments: This peak is connected to nearby Mt. Flume, and though it is not above treeline, offers good views from its rocky summit. A loop hike over the two summits is possible utilizing the Flume Slide, Franconia Ridge and Liberty Spring trails (7.3 mi.). Descending via the Flume Slide Trail is not recommended.

Flume (23)

Elevation: 4328 ft./1319 m.

USGS Quad/Coordinates: 7.4' Lincoln: 44N06/71W38.

Best Maps: AMC #5 - Franconia, Preston's Washington and Lafayette Trail Maps, DeLorme's Trail Map and Guide to the White Mountain National Forest.

Access: From Franconia Notch Parkway (I-93), Kancamagus Highway (NH 112).

Trails to Summit: Liberty Spring/Flume Slide/Franconia Ridge trails (4 mi.), Wilderness

/Osseo/Franconia Ridge trails (5.6 mi.).
Comments: The rocky and craggy summit of this peak has a precipitous eastern cliff, overlooking the slide that the Flume Slide Trail utilizes. This trail is very steep and potentially dangerous because it is wet. Descending on this trail is not recommended. The newly relocated Osseo Trail climbs the ridge from east and offers interesting views.

West of the Franconia Range

Cannon (24)

Elevation: 4077 ft./1250 m.
USGS Quad/Coordinates: 7.5' Franconia: 44N09/71W42.
Best Maps: AMC #5 - Franconia, Preston's Washington and Lafayette Trail Maps, DeLorme's Trail Map and Guide to the White Mountain National Forest.
Access: From Franconia Notch Parkway (I-93).
Trails to Summit: Kinsman Ridge Trail (2.1 mi.), Hi-Cannon Trail to Kinsman Ridge Trail (2.4 mi.).
Comments: Famous for the "Old Man of the Mountain" profile on its eastern face, this mountain also supports a major, state-operated ski area. There is a tramway that extends to just below the summit. A parking area is located near the bottom of this tramway.

North Kinsman (24)

Elevation: 4293 ft./1309 m.
USGS Quad/Coordinates: 7.5' Franconia: 44N08/71W44.
Best Maps: AMC #5 - Franconia, Preston's Washington and Lafayette Trail Maps, DeLorme's Trail Map and Guide to the White Mountain National Forest.
Access: From Franconia Notch Parkway (I-93) or near the Franconia/Easton town line south of NH 18.
Trails to Summit: Lonesome Lake, Cascade Brook, Fishin' Jimmy trails to Kinsman Ridge Trail (4 mi.). Appalachian Trail: Cascade Brook to Fishin' Jimmy to Kinsman Ridge trails (5.3 mi.), Mt. Kinsman Trail (4.1 mi.).
Comments: The summit is wooded but there are overlooks with excellent

views to the east out to the Franconia Range. The two Kinsmans stand opposite the exceptionally scenic Franconia Range and above Lonesome Lake and the AMC Lonesome Lake hut. Several trails in the area offer variations on the routes to the summit listed above.

South Kinsman (24)

Elevation: 4358 ft./1328 m.
USGS Quad/Coordinates: 7.5 Lincoln: 44N07/71W44.
Best Maps: AMC #5 - Franconia, Preston's Washington and Lafayette Trail Maps, DeLorme's Trail Map and Guide to the White Mountain National Forest.
Access: See North Kinsman.
Trails to Summit: See North Kinsman.
Comments: South Kinsman is located just one mile south of North Kinsman along the Kinsman Ridge Trail. The summit is open and plateau-like with good views. It is most easily climbed via the routes for North Kinsman.

Moosilauke (25)

Elevation: 4802 ft./1464 m.
USGS Quad/Coordinates: 7.5' Mt. Moosilauke: 44N01/71W50. **Best Maps:** AMC #5 - Franconia, Preston's Washington and Lafayette Trail Maps, DeLorme's Trail Map and Guide to the White Mountain National Forest.
Access: From NH 112, NH 116 or Glencliff.
Trails to Summit: From NH 112: Beaver Brook Trail (AT) (3.4 mi.). From Forest Road 147: Benton Trail (3.6 mi.). From off NH 118: Gorge Brook Trail (3.7 mi.), From off NH 25: Glencliff Trail (AT) (3.9 mi.).
Comments: The alpine summit area of this huge, rounded mountain is an immense field of grasses and rocks. Large stone cairns mark the route to the summit from the south, an old carriage road. The foundation of a former summit hotel is located near the summit. Many trails ascend the mountain including the 5 mi. Moosilauke Carriage Road.

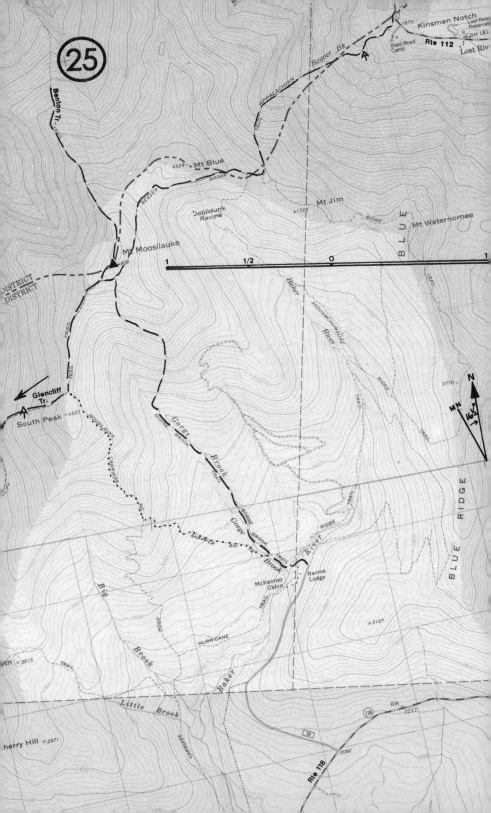

The broad, flat summit of Moosilauke

Additional Peaks of the New England Hundred Highest
in New Hampshire

Mountain	Elevation: ft/m	USGS Quad
Nancy	3906/1191	Crawford Notch
The Horn	3905/1190	Percy
Weeks	3890/1186	Mt. Washington
Weeks, South Peak	3885/1184	Mt. Washington
Vose Spur (Mt. Carrigain)	3870/1180	Crawford Notch
The Sleepers, East Peak	3850/1173	Mt. Chocorua
Nubble Peak		
(North Ridge of North Twin)	3813/1162	South Twin Mt.
Scar Ridge	3774/1150	Mt. Osceola
Cannon Bals, N.E. Peak	3769/1149	Franconia

Franconia Range from Osceola

Chapter 4

The Green Mountains of Vermont

Green Mountain Geology

The long Green Mountain range of Vermont contrasts sharply with the asymmetrical clustering of the White Mountains and the Adirondacks. These ancient mountains, the oldest standing mountains in this guide, form a long north/south ridge that is the spine of the state of Vermont. They probably once stood much higher than they are now -- it is said that about six miles elevation of rock has already been eroded from them.

The origins of this range are those of the main bulk of the eastern Appalachians. In early Paleozoic time (about 350 million years ago), a deep trough or syncline existed where the Green Mountains are located now. Silts and sands eroding from mountains and highlands to the east (which no longer exist) gradually filled the trough which sank deeper and deeper into the earth as the weight of the deposits increased. Pressured by the weight of accumulated sediments from above and subjected to heat from below, these sedimentary rocks were transformed into schists and other metamorphic rocks. Later, the mass was uplifted and the upper layers of rock were worn down. This process exposed the ancient roots that make up the present-day Green Mountains.

Glaciation further shaped the Green Mountains in similar ways as elsewhere in New England. There are rugged cliffs on the southern faces of a few mountains where the southward-moving glacial ice sheet plucked off huge boulders. Along the ridges are found glacial erratics, solitary boulders that were transported by the ice sheet. There is also plenty of polished bedrock marked by the scratches that these erratics and other boulders made in the rock as they were dragged along under the ice.

Vermont Hiking Clubs

All of the high summits in the Green Mountains are traversed by the Long Trail, the focus of activity for the Green Mountain Club (GMC). This group, founded in 1910, publishes the frequently updated *Guide Book of the Long Trail*. Topographic maps in the book show the Long Trail as well as many side trails. The GMC also publishes separate maps for Camel's Hump and Mt. Mansfield and a set of topographic maps of the entire Long Trail. The GMC is a large club and has chapters in states outside of Vermont. Their current headquarters is in Waterbury, Vermont.

Land Ownership and Management

Most of the Green Mountains are protected by the National Forest Service (Green Mountain National Forest) or the State of Vermont which owns large portions of Mt. Mansfield and all of Camel's Hump. Ski areas also own portions of mountains, though many of these fall within the constraints of the Forest Service boundaries.

The Green Mountains

Mountain	Elevation:ft/m	Date(s) Climbed
1. Mansfield	4393/1339	_____
2. Killington	4235/1291	_____
3. Camel's Hump	4083/1244	_____
4. Ellen	4083/1244	_____
5. Abraham	4006/1221	_____
6. Pico Peak	3957/1206	_____
7. Stratton	3936/1200	_____

The Chin, Mt. Mansfield's highest summit

DIRECTORY OF GREEN MOUNTAIN HIGH SUMMITS

Mount Mansfield (26)

Elevation: 4393 ft./1339 m.
USGS Quad: 15' Mt. Mansfield, 7.5' Mt. Mansfield: 44N33/72W49.
Best Maps: GMC Mt. Mansfield Region, GMC End to End #17.
Access: East, from VT 108 at or near Smuggler's Notch, west from Underhill State Park Campgrounds. North and south from the Long Trail.
Trails to Summit: Numerous, described in GMC Guide Book of the Long Trail. From VT 108: Long Trail (2.3 mi.), Hell Brook Trail to Long Trail (1.9 mi.). From Underhill State Park Campgrounds: Laura Cowles, Sunset Ridge trails to Long Trail (2.7 mi.).
Comments: Mt. Mansfield, the highest summit in Vermont, has a long, bare summit that is above treeline. With its numerous trails, ski slopes and lifts (on its eastern face), it attracts many hikers and visitors year round. A toll road to the summit ridge where a hotel used to stand, and a gondola from the ski area, brings thousands of tourists to the mountain's ridge many of whom walk the last mile to the true summit. The summit ridge near the toll road is also the location for a television station.

The bare summit of Mt. Mansfield contains much fragile arctic vegetation and hikers are advised to walk only on marked trails or bare rock outcrops. When viewed from afar, the summit ridge is seen to have the features of a face looking skyward and the several summits have been named accordingly. The highest summit, north of and well away from all the development, is the "chin." The eastern face of Mt. Mansfield is steep and contains a number of cliffs over which some of the trails climb.

Camel's Hump (27)

Elevation: 4083 ft./1245 m.
USGS Quad: 15' Camel's Hump, 7.5' Huntington, 7.5' Waterbury: 44N19/72W53. **Best Maps:** GMC Camel's Hump Area, GMC End to End #15.
Access: Camel's Hump State Park. From the east: roughly south of I-89/west of VT 100. Off River Road west of Waterbury. From the west: Huntington Center.
Trails to Summit: Long Trail north and south, From the east: Forestry

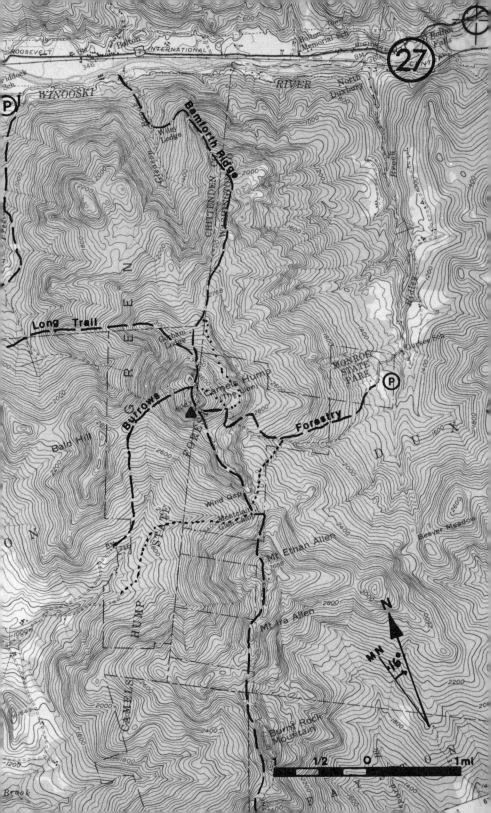

Looking north to Camel's Hump from the Long Trail

Trail (3.4 mi.) From the west: Burrows Trail (2.7 mi.). From the north: Bamforth Ridge Trail to Long Trail (5.9 mi.).

Comments: Camel's Hump is the only major peak in Vermont that has not been disturbed by ski development. The summit itself is a bare cone that contains a fragile arctic/alpine community of plants. Please stay on the trail to protect this ecosystem. Camel's Hump is heavily used by hikers and its small summit can actually be crowded at certain times of the year.

Ellen (28)
See also (29)

Elevation: 4083 ft./1245 m.
USGS Quad: 7.5' Mt. Ellen: 44N09/72W53.
Best Maps: GMC End to End #14.
Access: from Lincoln Gap between Warren and Lincoln. From VT 17.
Trails to Summit: Long Trail north from Lincoln Gap (6.3 mi.). Long Trail south from VT 17 (5.3 mi.). A western approach from off VT 17 is possible also using the Jerusalem Trail to the Long Trail south (4.3 mi.).
Comments: Mt. Ellen is one of two summits on Lincoln Mountain (the other is Mt. Abraham) that lie over 4,000 ft. and are separated from other high points on the ridge by a 200 ft. col. Lincoln Mountain is a long north/south ridge that supports a number of ski operations on its eastern face. The actual summit of Mt. Ellen is wooded, but there are views from Cutts Peak just .4 miles south and some from the ski trails.

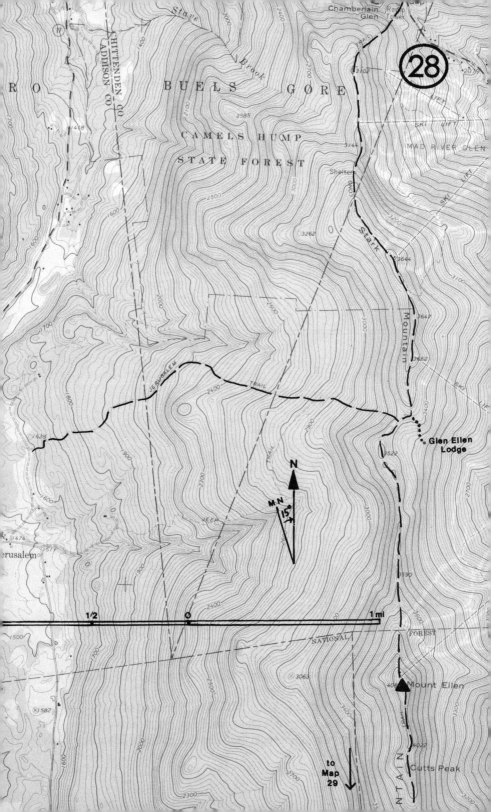

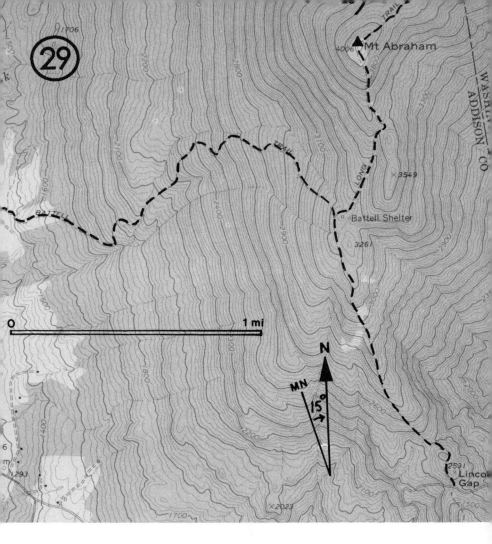

Abraham (29)
See also (28)

Elevation: 4006 ft./1221 m.
USGS Quad: 7.5' Mt. Ellen, 7.5' Lincoln: 44N07/72W56.
Best Maps: GMC End to End #13.
Access: From Lincoln Gap between Warren and Lincoln.
Trails to Summit: Long Trail north from Lincoln Gap (2.6 mi.). Battell Trail to Long Trail north (2.9 mi.).
Comments: Along with Mt. Ellen, Mt. Abraham is one of the two highest summits along the Lincoln Mountain ridge. Its summit is bare and supports some fragile alpine vegetation that can be easily damaged. Please

stay on the marked trail. Below and south of the summit is the Long Trail Battell Shelter.

Pico Peak (30)

Elevation: 3957 ft./1206 m.
USGS Quad: 7.5' Pico Peak, 7.5' Killington: 43N38/72W50.
Best Maps: GMC End to End #9.
Access: From US 4 - Sherburne Pass. **Trails to Summit:** Long Trail/AT south to Pico Link Trail (2.9 mi.).
Comments: The conical summit of this peak has been marred by the ski area, but there are plenty of views through the ski trail cuts. Just below the summit, and connected to it by the Pico Link Trail, is the Pico Camp cabin. The Long Trail between Pico Peak and Killington skirts the western edge of the ridge between these peaks.

Killington (30)

Elevation: 4241 ft./1293 m.
USGS Quad: 7.5' Killington: 43N36/72W49.
Best Maps: GMC End to End #9.
Access: from US 4 - Sherburne Pass, Wheelerville Road south of US 4, or VT 100.

Appalachian Trail "through-hikers" on the summit of Killington

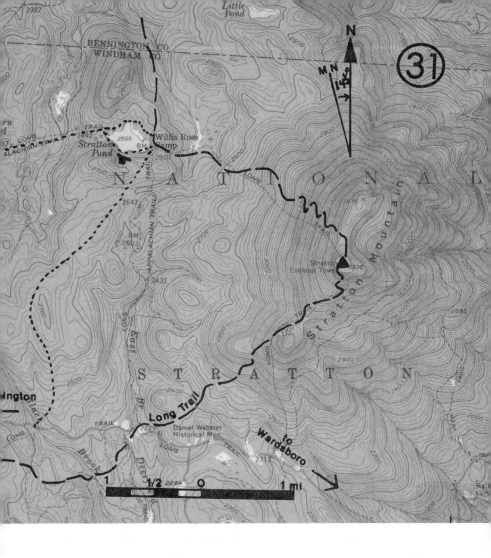

Stratton Mountain from Stratton Pond

Trails to Summit: Long Trail/AT south from Sherburne Pass (5.4 mi.). Bucklin Trail from Wheelerville Road (3.4 mi.). From VT 100: Black Swamp Trail to Shrewsbury Peak Trail to Long Trail north (4.7 mi.).

Comments: Killington, the second highest summit in Vermont, is a popular skier's mountain, with its entire eastern side transformed for that sport. The summit itself is rock and affords a 360-degree view. There are radio installations and towers on the summit that, together with the ski development, detract from its rugged nature. Just below and south of the summit is Cooper Lodge, a shelter with bunks for 12 to 16. Mendon Peak, one of the New England Hundred Highest, is nearby to the southwest. Shrewsbury Peak to the southeast offers good views. Killington may also be climbed via one of its many ski trails.

Stratton (31)

Elevation: 3936 ft./1200 m.
USGS Quad: 15' Londonderry: 43N05/72W55.
Best Maps: GMC End to End #4.
Access: Arlington/Wardsboro Road.
Trails to Summit: Long Trail/AT north and south.
Comments: Technically, Stratton has been measured to be a foot shy of the 1200 meter limit used in this book. It is a big mountain that stands by itself, the most southerly high peak in New England, and so close to the limit that it has been included in the list. Who knows what a future survey might do with this 1' difference? It is also important as the mountain on which James P. Taylor conceived of the Long Trail and Benton MacKaye conceived of the Appalachian Trail. On its wooded southern summit is a large observation tower, and on the lower northern summit a ski area. Stratton Pond, with two shelters and a camping area, is below and west of the summit.

Additional Peaks of the New England Hundred Highest in Vermont

Mountain	Elevation: ft/m	USGS Quad
Jay Peak	3861/1177	Jay Peak
Equinox	3840/1170	Manchester
Mendon Peak	3840/1170	Killington
Bread Loaf	3835/1169	Lincoln
Big Jay	3800/1158	Jay Peak
Wilson	3790/1155	Lincoln
Dorset Peak	3760/1146	Dorset

Chapter 5

The Adirondacks of New York State

The Geology of the Adirondacks

Unlike the Green Mountains, the White Mountains and the Catskills, the Adirondacks are not part of the great Appalachian chain. The Adirondack mountains are something different -- and they are both old and new. Geologists consider them to be part of a range that extends northward and includes Quebec's Laurentian Range. A major rocky type in the Adirondacks is anorthosite, a very old metamorphic rock that originated about 1.1 billion years ago. Anorthosite is a rock that was chemically altered (like other metamorphic and igneous rocks) by extreme heat and pressure in its creation far beneath the surface of the earth. Because the rock was formed in one semi-molten mass, it doesn't exhibit joints, fracture lines or bedding planes, and it's not uncommon to come upon wide expanses of it where no plants are able to grab a root hold. Anorthosite "exfoliates" (more or less peels) as it weathers, leaving large slabs sitting over the solid bedrock. This weathering characteristic is the reason behind the immense slides found on many Adirondack mountains, slides that often extend from summit to valley, and are only very gradually reclaimed by vegetation.

In some places in the Adirondacks, natural fractures in the rock were filled by molten igneous rock, forming dikes of diabase and metamorphosed gabbro. These can be observed as dark bands, some of which are so wide that they have directed the course of streams. The great dike on Mt. Colden is one of the best known dikes in the High Peaks region of the Adirondacks.

While anorthosite is old, the mountains themselves are relatively young. They started as basement rocks for an ancient mountain range, one that possibly stood as tall as today's Himalayas, but they were never near the surface. Over time, though, the rock above them eroded and was carried away. About 50 million years ago, the land experienced an uplift which accelerated erosion. Eventually, the Adirondack mass was exposed; by resisting the erosion that was wearing down the softer rocks around it, mountains "emerged." Sculpting by glacial ice during the ice ages completed the work that has resulted in their present appearance. Ancient faults have been washed and scoured out, producing what appears to be ranges of summits. These are relatively young mountains when compared with the 350-million-year age of the Appalachians. Evidence suggests that they are still rising.

The anorthosite that makes up the Adirondacks links them to an ancient part of the earth's crust known as the Canadian Shield. They are one of only a few places where the basement rocks of the continent poke up above the surface. In essence, the Adirondacks are part of the underlying structure of the North American continent, the solid platform on which everything else rests.

Hiking Clubs in the Adirondacks

The Adirondack Mountain Club (ADK), founded in 1922, publishes a series of guides to the Adirondacks, including *Guide to Adirondack Trails: High Peaks Region*. They also publish an excellent map of this area that comes with this guide or can be purchased separately. The ADK has chapters throughout New York State and one in New Jersey that all organize hikes for members throughout the year. Members receive their bi-monthly magazine "Adirondack."

The Adirondack Forty-Sixers is the classic peakbagging club. Inspired by the climbs of Robert and George Marshall, and Herbert Clark, the Forty-Sixers of Troy, NY was organized in 1937 as the first peakbagging club. During the 1940s members of this group felt the need for a more specific organization comprised of only those who had completed climbs of all 46 Adirondack peaks then thought to be over 4,000 feet. In 1948, the Adirondack Forty-Sixers came into being and an emblem was adopted. The Forty-Sixers publishes the semi-annual "Adirondack Peeks" which contains stories and photos of hiking experiences in the Adirondacks, as well as news about the area.

Adirondack Trailheads

The High Peaks region of the Adirondacks is not so easily divided into ranges as are the White Mountains, and there are no roads that cut across the central part of the mountainous mass. Most of the summits are approached from a few key trailheads, which are listed below.

1. **Adirondack Loj**, at the end of paved Heart Lake Road which starts

south of NY 73, about 3 miles east of Lake Placid and 11 miles west of Keene. (Adirondack Loj was named by Melville Dewey, inventor of the Dewey Decimal System, who was also an advocate of simplified spelling). Besides the lodge, there is a large parking lot here owned and managed by the Adirondack Mountain Club. (fee charged - $6/day in 1992). This is a very popular approach to the High Peaks, and the lot may be full on weekends during summer. An alternative is to park or camp at South Meadow, reached via South Meadow Road, which leaves Heart Lake Road about 3 miles south of NY 73 and about a mile before Adirondack Loj. This dirt road reaches South Meadow in about a mile, passing many camping areas along the way. This area is connected by a service road to Marcy Dam and trails to Adirondack Loj and Johns Brook Lodge.

Marcy Dam, which has created a small, beautiful pond with mountains rising impressively behind it, is an important hub of the High Peaks trail system and a very popular camping place. It can be reached by a 2.3 mile trail from Adirondack Loj or by the service road (foot travel only) from South Meadow. Located here is the Marcy Dam DEC Interior Outpost (ranger station).

2. **The Garden** is 1.6 miles from NY 73 from the center of the town of Keene Valley. This parking area, limited to about 55 cars, allows hikers access to the Great Range, Marcy, Big Slide and others. The lot usually fills up during weekends and overflow parking is not allowed near the trailhead. You may be able to arrange transportation to this major trailhead if you stay at one of the inns or bed & breakfasts in Keene Valley. About 3 miles from the Garden along a relatively flat trail that follows Johns Brook is a ranger station, the Johns Brook DEC Interior Outpost. There are several campsites in this vicinity. Johns Brook Lodge (JBL) and cabins, maintained by the ADK and open to the public, are about a half mile farther along this trail.

3. **Adirondack Mountain Reserve (AMR)**, a.k.a. the Ausable Club, is a private holding within the High Peaks region of Adirondack Park. It lies in a dramatic fault valley that contains the East Branch of the Ausable River and Upper and Lower Ausable Lakes. At the head of the valley is the town of Saint Huberts on NY 73. Some members of this private club founded the Adirondack Trail Improvement Society (ATIS) and built a number of trails, most of which are open to the public today. Hikers are restricted to certain trails and are forbidden to hike off the trails or to camp

Top: Haystack from Basin
Bottom: Colden (near) and the MacIntyre Range from Marcy

on Club land, which is clearly marked on the ADK map and by signs on trails where they cross the Club boundaries. Dogs (or other pets) are forbidden to use the parts of trails that cross Club land. Hikers should remember that this is private land that has been graciously opened to public use under these restrictions; the AMR regulations are strictly enforced. Hikers who wish to use this approach to the peaks that surround this valley, including the Colvin and Great Ranges, must enter the area via Lake Road, which begins at the St. Huberts Inn and ends at the club boathouse on Lower Ausable Lake. Hiker parking is restricted to a small lot at the trailhead parking for Noonmark and Round Mountain located 3/4 mile east of the Inn and about 1/4 mile from NY 73. It is a long walk to some of the trailheads and one option during the summer months is to take the hourly bus. This bus, which primarily serves members, will take hikers (if seating is available) to and from specific hiker bus stops for $3.00 exact change (in 1992) each way. Lake Road is about four miles long and can be walked in about 1.5 hours. One other option is to hike into the area using one of the two trails that follow the East Branch of the Ausable River.

On the north end of remote Upper Ausable Lake is the Warden's Camp from which several trails originate. This is a base from which the private land of the AMR is patrolled. Hikers are allowed to use many of the trails that pass through the Upper Ausable Lake area, but since there is no trail along the valley from Lake Road, hikers must first climb over one of the surrounding High Peaks and then descend to Upper Ausable Lake. This is a strenuous trip made more difficult by the fact that camping is not permitted on AMR land, forcing backpackers to camp on state land which requires a substantial climb from the lake to one's campsite.

4. **Elk Lake**, the setting for privately owned Elk Lake Lodge, is a large lake that marks a southeastern approach to the High Peaks. From Northway Exit 29 take Blue Ridge Road west, turn right (north) after four miles and find the parking area and trailheads about 5 miles ahead on this road. Before reaching state land, many of the trails in this area cross private land where hikers are required to stay on the trails.

5. **Tahawus/Upper Works** is the general term for an area where several trailheads are located along the old Tahawus Club Road on the southwestern edge of the High Peaks. This area has a long history of mining activity. It was the site of the old MacIntyre iron works, and some of the old buildings, including a large stone furnace, still stand and can be

seen from the road. More recently, the National Lead Company operated a titanium mine (presently inactive) at Sanford Lake where the old Tahawus Club Road ends; large piles of tailings are visible throughout the area. The Tahawus Club itself, historically famous as the place where Vice-President Theodore Roosevelt was vacationing when he was notified of the imminent death of President McKinley, was displaced by the mining operations; several of its abandoned buildings also remain standing. The 10-mile drive to the last trailhead is located off Blue Ridge Road roughly 17 miles west of Northway Exit 29.

Approximately midway between Upper Works and Adirondack Loj, at the southern end of Lake Colden, is the Lake Colden DEC Interior Outpost (ranger station).

6. **Coreys Road**, south of NY 3, is the main northwest entrance to the High Peaks. Many of the trails in the area, flat and uninteresting to hikers, are designed and primarily used for horse travel. Peakbaggers will use these trails, however, to approach the Seward Range.

Land Ownership and Management in the Adirondacks

Most of the Adirondack High Peaks region lies within the boundaries of the Adirondack Forest Preserve. It is state law that the lands within these boundaries remain "forever wild." Some trails do cross private land, however, where hikers are customarily forbidden to hike off trail or to camp. The ADK High Peaks Region map shows these boundaries.

Trails in the Adirondacks

Trails in the Adirondacks are not arranged in the most logical fashion. The naming of trails, their continuity and intersections with other trails, and their different colored markings can seem confusing. Most trails in the High Peaks region are maintained by the New York state Department of Conservation (DEC). These trails are marked with circular metal tags of varying colors. A good number of other trails are maintained by the Adirondack Mountain Club (ADK) or the Adirondack Trail Improvement Society (ATIS), both of which use red metal tags. On the so-called trailless peaks are unmarked and unmaintained trails called "herd paths." These can be very rough, requiring you to dodge sharp branches, crawl under blowdowns and wade through deep black mud. To some this is a joy, to others an experience that increases their respect for trail maintenance. Above treeline, cairns (stone piles) or paint marks usually mark the route. Some trails in the Adirondacks receive very heavy use and during wet periods become reduced to black mud. Consider bringing extra footwear, such as a pair of sneakers or flip-flops, for in-camp use when planning a trip.

New York's Adirondack Mountains

Mountain	Elevation: ft/m*	Date(s) Climbed
1. Marcy	5344/1629	_____
2. Algonquin	5115/1559	_____
3. Haystack	4961/1512	_____
4. Skylight	4925/1501	_____
5. Whiteface	4865/1483	_____
6. Iroquois	4849/1478	_____
7. Dix	4839/1470+	_____
8. Gray	4826/1471	_____
9. Basin	4826/1471	_____
10. Gothics	4734/1443	_____
11. Colden	4715/1437	_____
12. Giant	4626/1410	_____
13. Nippletop	4609/1400+	_____
14. Santanoni	4606/1404	_____
15. Redfield	4606/1404	_____
16. Wright	4587/1398	_____
17. Saddleback	4528/1380	_____
18. Armstrong	4445/1350+	_____
19. Panther	4442/1354	_____
20. Tabletop	4413/1345	_____
21. Hough	4409/1344	_____
22. Macomb	4390/1338	_____
23. Rocky Peak Ridge	4383/1336	_____
24. Marshall	4379/1330+	_____
25. Allen	4347/1325	_____
26. Seward	4347/1320+	_____
27. Big Slide	4248/1290+	_____
28. Esther	4239/1292	_____
29. Upper Wolf Jaw	4203/1281	_____

30. Lower Wolf Jaw	4173/1272	_____
31. Phelps	4160/1268	_____
32. Street	4150/1260+	_____
33. Sawteeth	4150/1260+	_____
34. Donaldson	4108/1252	_____
35. Cascade	4098/1249	_____
36. Seymour	4091/1247	_____
37. South Dix	4084/1240+	_____
38. Porter	4084/1240+	_____
39. Colvin	4084/1240+	_____
40. Emmons	4039/1231	_____
41. Dial	4019/1220+	_____
42. East Dix	4006/1221	_____
43. MacNaughton	3983/1214	_____
44. Blake	3986/1210+	_____
45. Green	3960/1207	_____
46. Cliff	3944/1202	_____
47. Nye	3887/1180+	_____
48. Couchsachraga	3793/1156	_____

Elevations followed by (+) are based on the highest contour line of the latest USGS topographic maps. These latest USGS maps, released in 1978 and 1979, have contour intervals of 10 meters (about 32.8 feet apart) and do not give an exact summit figure for the 14 summits noted. In the elevation column above, the figure in meters is the highest contour on the USGS map; the figure in feet is an estimated number determined by adding half the contour interval to the highest contour. The 14 summits noted above may, therefore, be up to 16 feet higher or lower than the listed elevation in feet. These figures (which change the previous ranking of peaks based on the 1950's maps) were taken from Appendix B in "Of the Summits, of the Forests" published by the Adirondack Forty-Sixers.

Basin from Skylight

DIRECTORY OF ADIRONDACK HIGH PEAKS

Whiteface Mountain (32)

Elevation: 4865 ft./1483 m.
USGS Quad/Coordinates: 15' Lake Placid: 44N22/73W55.
Best Maps: ADK Trails of the Adirondack High Peaks Region.
Access: Wilmington: Whiteface Memorial Highway. Connery Pond via Whiteface Landing.
Trails to Summit: Wilmington Trail (5.2 mi.). Connery Pond/Whiteface Landing trails (6 mi.).
Comments: With its world-class ski area and its road leading nearly to the summit, on which a weather station and an observation house are located, Whiteface Mountain is by far the most developed of all the high peaks in the Adirondacks. Its summit area is above treeline, permitting views in all directions.

Esther Mountain (32)

Elevation: 4239 ft./1292 m.
USGS Quad/Coordinates: 15' Lake Placid: 44N23/73W54.
Best Maps: ADK Trails of the Adirondack High Peaks Region.
Access: Wilmington: Whiteface Memorial Highway.
Trails to Summit: No official trail; the summit is usually reached from the Wilmington Trail on a herd path over the summit of Lookout Mt. Total distance is about 4.7 mi.
Comments: Mt. Esther was named for Esther McComb who, in 1839 at the age of 15, got disoriented while trying to climb Whiteface. She got lost on the summit of Esther and had to be rescued the next day.

Cascade Mountain (33)

Elevation 4098 ft./1249 m.
USGS Quad/Coordinates: 15' Mt. Marcy: 44N13/73W52.
Best Maps: ADK Trails of the High Peaks Region. Discover the Adirondack High Peaks.
Access: NY 73 west of Cascade Lakes.

Trails to Summit: Cascade Trail (2.4 mi.).

Comments: The rocky, conical summit of this mountain, with its excellent views, its convenient access from Route 73, and the relative ease of the climb, makes Cascade one of the most climbed of the High Peaks. A large cascade between the lakes gives this mountain its name. Nearby Porter Mt. is often included in a climb to Cascade.

Porter Mountain (33)

Elevation: 4084 ft./1240+ m.

USGS Quad/Coordinates: 15' Mt. Marcy: 44N12/73W51.

Best Maps: ADK Trails of the High Peaks Region. Discover the Adirondack High Peaks.

Access: NY 73 west of Cascade Lakes. The Garden at Keene Valley. NY 73 near Keene Valley Airport.

Trails to Summit: Cascade Trail (2.8 mi.). Porter Trail over Little Porter Mtn. from Johns Brook Road (4 mi.). Ridge Trail over Blueberry Mtn. from airport (4.5 mi.).

Comments: This peak is usually climbed along with Cascade, just .7 miles to the northwest, via the Cascade Trail. The other two routes approach the summit from the east. They are longer and require more elevation gain, but they are also less traveled and more scenic. Although its summit is partially wooded, there are views from near the summit. Porter was named for Noah Porter, a president of Yale University, who led the first recorded ascent of the mountain in 1875. Previously it was known as West Mountain.

Big Slide Mountain (34)

Elevation: 4248 ft./1290+ m.

USGS Quad/Coordinates: 15' Mt. Marcy: 44N11/73W53.

Best Maps: ADK Trails of the High Peaks Region. Discover the Adirondack High Peaks.

Access: The Garden at Keene Valley. Johns Brook Lodge (JBL) area.

Trails to Summit: The Brothers Trail (3.9). Slide Mt. Brook Trail from JBL (2.4 mi.). Klondike Notch Trail from JBL (4 mi.).

Comments: This mountain is named for the large slide on its eastern face. The partial view from its summit, mostly to the east and south, takes in a stunning panorama of the Great Range from the Wolfjaws to Marcy. The

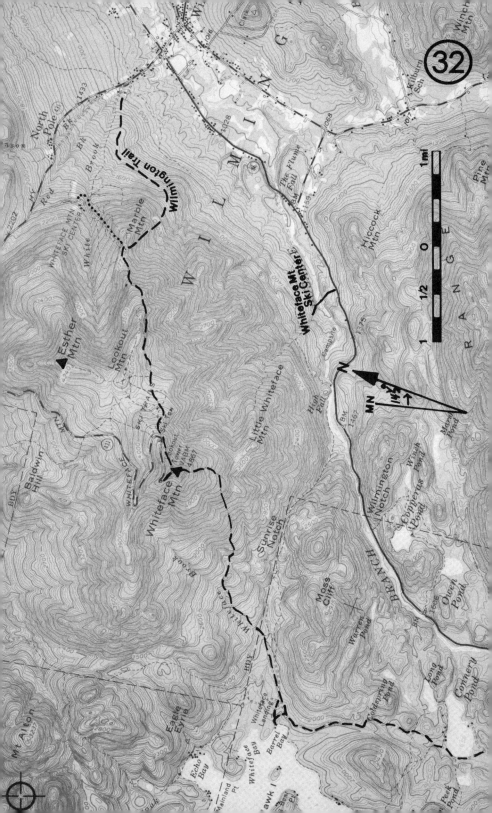

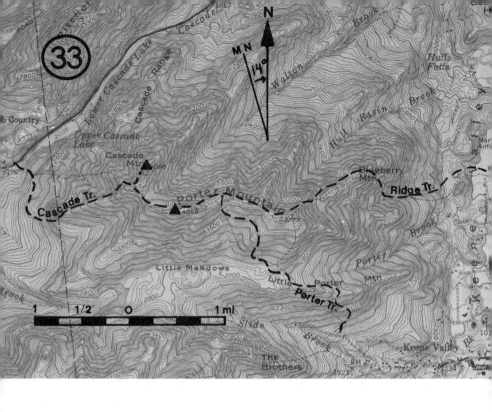

climb to Big Slide over the Brothers (Brothers Trail from the Garden) is routed along open ledges with excellent views. The other two routes start at Johns Brook Lodge, a 3.5 mi. hike from the Garden via the Phelps Trail. The lodge, owned by the Adirondack Mountain Club, is a convenient focal point for climbs to the summits in the area because several trails start within a short distance of it. (Note: there are several other buildings owned by the ADK nearby.)

On the way to Giant's summit

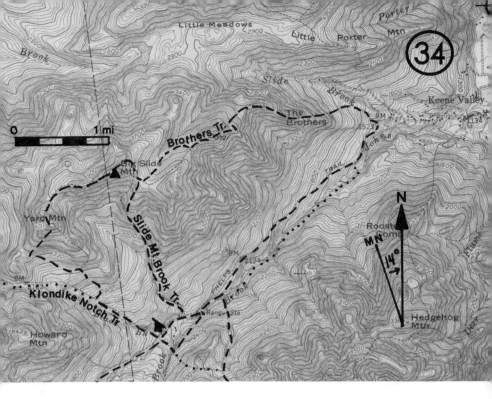

Giant Wilderness Area

Green Mountain (35)

Elevation: 3960 ft./1207 m.
USGS Quad/Coordinates: 15' Elizabethtown, 15' Mt. Marcy: 44N11/73W43. **Best Maps:** ADK Trails of the High Peaks Region.
Access: NY 73 near Saint Huberts. NY 9N.
Trail to Summit: None.
Comments: Because Green Mountain has never been found to be over 4,000 ft. it is not often climbed. It is, however, higher than Cliff, Nye and Couchsachraga, all of which must be climbed for Forty Sixer membership. There is a trail that runs through the valley between it and Giant from which a climb to its flat, wooded summit may be attempted. (see Conroy, Dawson and McMartin, *Discover the Northeastern Adirondacks,* Backcountry Publications, p. 96)

Giant Mountain (35)

Elevation: 4626 ft./1410 m.
USGS Quad/Coordinates: 15' Mount Marcy, 15' Elizabethtown: 44N10/73W43.

Best Maps: ADK Trails of the High Peaks Region.
Access: From NY 73 near Chapel Pond. NY 73 near Saint Huberts. From NY 9 south of New Russia. From NY 9N.
Trails to Summit: Ridge Trail from near Chapel Pond (3 mi.). Roaring Brook Trail from Saint Huberts (3.6 mi.). East Trail via Rocky Peak Ridge (8 mi.). North Trail from NY 9N (7.4 mi.).
Comments: Giant may have been the first major peak in the Adirondacks to be climbed -- in 1797 by Charles Broadhead the surveyor. The full name for this peak, a massive mountain with a glacial cirque on its western face, is Giant of the Valley. The climb to its summit requires an elevation gain of at least 3,000 feet, much more if approached from the east. A number of expansive open ledges offer views to the north on the ascent from Chapel Pond. The summit offers views in all directions.

Rocky Peak Ridge (35)

Elevation: 4383 ft./1336 m.
USGS Quad/Coordinates: 15' Elizabethtown, 15' Mt. Marcy: 44N09/73W43.
Best Maps: ADK Trails of the High Peaks Region.
Access: From NY 9 (south of New Russia) or from the shoulder of Giant Mtn.
Trails to Summit: East Trail (5.4 mi.).
Comments: This ridge-like summit is moderately difficult to reach, requiring either a climb over Giant to the west, or a long hike over Bald Peak from NY 9 to the east. Just east of the summit is a glacial pond, Lake Marie Louise.

The Dix Range

Dix Mountain (36)

Elevation: 4839 ft./1470+ m.
USGS Quad/Coordinates: 15' Mt. Marcy: 44N05/73W47.
Best Maps: ADK Trails of the High Peaks Region. Discover the Adirondack High Peaks. **Access:** NY 73 near Saint Huberts. Elk Lake.
Trails to Summit: Dix trail from AMR (6.8 mi.). Dix via Hunters Pass trail (7.3 mi.).
Comments: This peak was named for John Adams Dix, public servant and

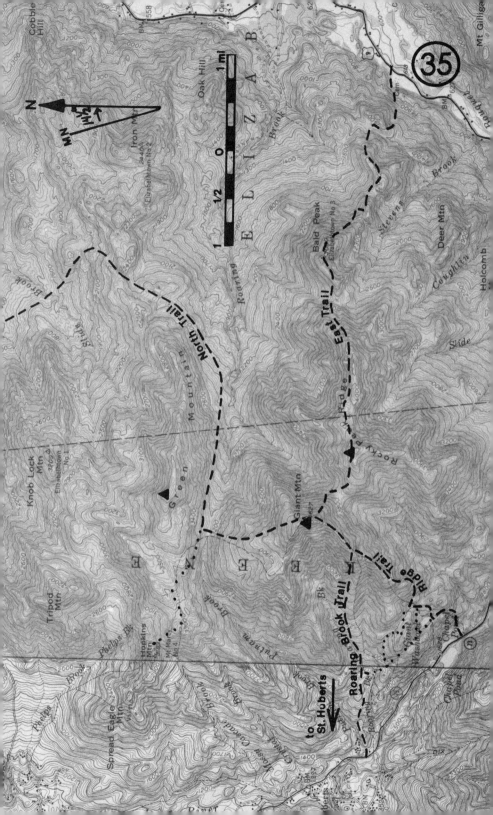

Atop the summit of Dix

general. He was elected governor of NY in 1872. The summit is an open narrow ridge with views in all directions. The two approaches to Dix, from St. Huberts and Elk Lake, are roughly equal in length, but the elevation gain from St. Huberts is greater.

Astute readers will notice that the elevation given for Dix is somewhat short of the 4857-ft. figure given in many guide books. The most recent USGS survey, published in the late 1970's, did not give Dix a specific elevation. The highest contour for the mountain on these maps is 1470 meters. In this books's listing, the elevation in feet is given as the midpoint between 1470 and 1480 meters. It is possible, however, that the peak may rise as much as 32 feet higher (just short of 1480 meters) which would bring it to 4855 ft. Since we don't know for sure, a listing of the highest contour in meters, followed by a (+), and a midpoint estimate in feet was chosen as the model for all situations of this kind. This is the method used by the AMC 4000-Footer Club for ranking peaks in the White Mountains and Maine. See the listing at the head of this section for other mountains affected in this way.

Hough Peak (36)

Elevation: 4409 ft./1344 m.
USGS Quad/Coordinates: 15' Mt. Marcy: 44N04/73W46.
Best Maps: ADK Trails of the High Peaks Region. Discover the Adirondack High Peaks.
Access: Elk Lake.
Trails to Summit: Herd path.

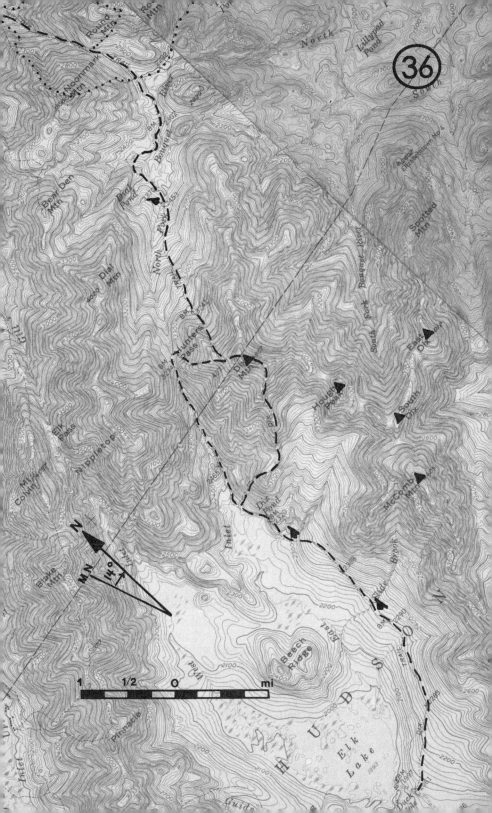

Comments: This peak was named for Franklin B. Hough, an historian and forester. It is technically trailless although a herd path from Dix Mtn. crosses its summit as well as those of South Dix and Macomb. There are views to the west from its summit.

East Dix (36)

Elevation: 4006 ft./1221 m.
USGS Quad/Coordinates: 15' Mt. Marcy: 44N04/73W45.
Best Maps: ADK Trails of the High Peaks Region. Discover the Adirondack High Peaks.
Access: Elk Lake. NY 73.
Trail to Summit: Herd path.
Comments: This summit is reached via a herd path from the summit of South Dix. View are good from the summit. There is also a route to the summit from NY 73 along the South Fork of the Bouquet River.

South Dix (36)

Elevation: 4084 ft./1240+ m.
USGS Quad/Coordinates: 15' Mt. Marcy: 44N03/73W46.
Best Maps: ADK Trails of the High Peaks Region. Discover the Adirondack High Peaks.
Access: Elk Lake.
Trail to Summit: Herd path.
Comments: A herd path from Macomb Mtn. runs to the wooded summit, with limited views. Ledges just south of the summit provide spectacular views.

Macomb Mountain (36)

Elevation: 4390 ft./1338 m.
USGS Quad/Coordinates: 15' Mt. Marcy: 44N03/73W46.
Best Maps: ADK Trails of the High Peaks Region. Discover the Adirondack High Peaks.
Access: Elk Lake.
Trail to Summit: Herd path from Slide Brook.
Comments: This mountain was probably named for General Alexander Macomb, victor in the Battle of Plattsburg in 1814. Two slides on the

western face of this mountain are utilized as part of the herd path routes to the open summit.

Adirondack Mountain Reserve Peaks and the Colvin Range

Dial Mountain (37)

Elevation: 4019 ft./1220+ m.
USGS Quad/Coordinates: 15' Mt. Marcy: 44N06/73W47.
Best Maps: ADK Trails of the High Peaks Region. Discover the Adirondack High Peaks.
Access: AMR/Lake Road.
Trail to Summit: Henry Goddard Leach Trail (3.8 mi.).
Comments: Along the wooded ridge line between Bear Den and Nippletop are the two high points of Dial Mountain; the one to the north has a viewpoint.

Blake and Colvin from Dix

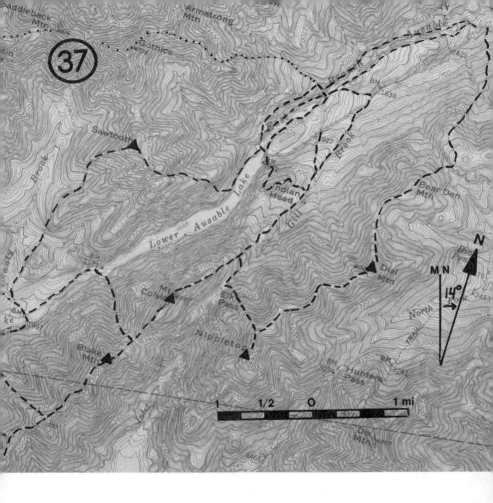

Nippletop (37)

Elevation: 4609 ft./1400+ m.
USGS Quad/Coordinates: 15' Mt. Marcy: 44N05/73W49.
Best Maps: ADK Trails of the High Peaks Region. Discover the Adirondack High Peaks.
Access: AMR/Lake Road.
Trails to Summit: Gill Brook Trail to Elk Pass (3.5 mi.). Henry Goddard Leach Trail via Dial (5.9 mi.).
Comments: Climbing Nippletop from either trail requires about 3,000-ft. elevation gain. The view of cliffs and wilderness from the summit is considered one of the best in the High Peaks.

Mt. Colvin (37)

Elevation: 4084 ft./1240+ m.
USGS Quad/Coordinates: 15' Mt. Marcy: 44N05/73W50.
Best Maps: ADK Trails of the High Peaks Region. Discover the Adirondack High Peaks.
Access: AMR/Lake Road.
Trail to Summit: Gill Brook trail (2.9 mi.). Comments: This peak was named after the great Adirondack surveyor and preservationist, Verplanck Colvin. The summit offers wide views and is the first high point on a long ridge called the Colvin Range which includes Blake and Pinnacle.

Blake Peak (37)

Elevation: 3986 ft./1210+ m.
USGS Quad/Coordinates: 15' Mt. Marcy: 44N05/73W51.
Best Maps: ADK Trails of the High Peaks Region. Discover the Adirondack High Peaks.
Access: AMR/Lake Road.
Trails to Summit: Gill Brook/Colvin trails.
Comments: This peak was once thought to be over 4,000 ft. so it made the Forty Sixer list. A later survey showed it lower than the sacred number -- but it still counts for club membership. Blake Peak was named for Verplanck Colvin's devoted friend and co-worker, Mills Blake. There are limited views from the summit, but there is an excellent view about 1/3 mile south of the summit along the trail to Pinnacle.

Sawteeth (37)

Elevation: 4150 ft./1260+ m.
USGS Quad/Coordinates: 15' Mt. Marcy: 44N07/73W51.
Best Maps: ADK Trails of the High Peaks Region. Discover the Adirondack High Peaks.
Access: AMR/Lake Road.
Trails to Summit: Alfred E. Weld Trail (to Gothics) to Sawteeth trail (2.2 mi.). Scenic Trail (3 mi.). A trail from Upper Ausable Lake/Warden's Camp also leads to the summit in about 3 miles.
Comments: Several jagged pinnacles, lined up like teeth on a saw, give this mountain its name. The climb up on the Scenic Trail passes several

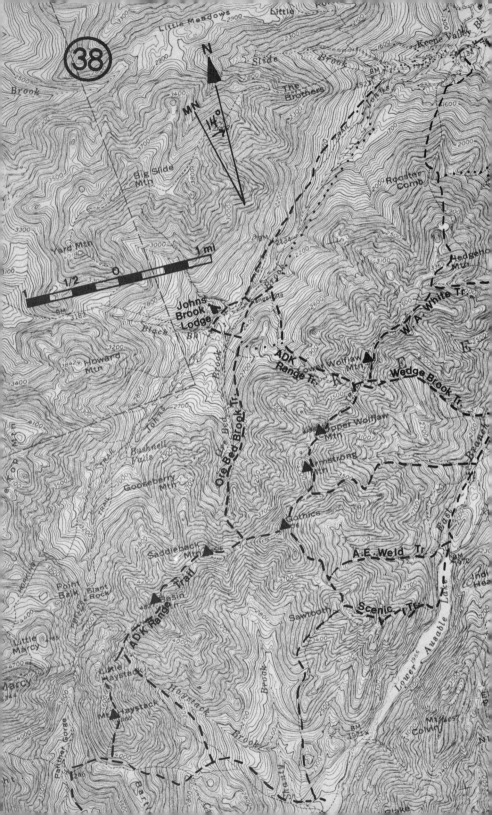

numbered overlooks before it reaches the wooded summit. There are also overlooks from the summit that offer excellent views, including one west to Gothics. The Alfred E. Weld Trail leads back to Lake Road, and combined with the Scenic Trail, makes for an interesting loop hike of about 5.5 mi. over the mountain.

The Great Range

Lower Wolf Jaw (38)

Elevation: 4173 ft./1272 m.
USGS Quad/Coordinates: 15' Mt. Marcy: 44N09/73W50.
Best Maps: ADK Trails of the High Peaks Region. Discover the Adirondack High Peaks.
Access: The Garden to Johns Brook DEC Interior Outpost (3.1 mi.). AMR/Lake Road.
Trails to Summit: ADK Range Trail from DEC Interior Outpost (2.5 mi.). Wedge Brook Trail (4.2 mi.). William A. White Trail (4.5 mi.).
Comments: Lower Wolf Jaw is the northernmost major summit along the Range Trail, the trail that follows the crest of the Great Range. Although the summit is wooded, there are views just below it.

The Great Range from Big Slide

Upper Wolf Jaw (38)

Elevation: 4203 ft./1281 m.
USGS Quad/Coordinates: 15' Mt. Marcy: 44N08/73W50.
Best Maps: ADK Trails of the High Peaks Region. Discover the Adirondack High Peaks.
Access: The Garden to Johns Brook DEC Interior Outpost (3.1 mi.). AMR/Lake Road.
Trails to Summit: ADK Range Trail from DEC Interior Outpost (2.9 mi.). Wedge Brook Trail (4.8 mi.).
Comments: From Wolf Jaw col, the ADK Range Trail leads south to a jagged ridge to the summit. There are many views along the way and at the summit. Both Upper and Lower Wolf Jaw may be climbed from either the Johns Brook Lodge area or from the Adirondack Mountain Reserve lands.

Armstrong Mountain (38)

Elevation: 4445 ft./1350+ m.
USGS Quad/Coordinates: 15' Mt. Marcy: 44N08/73W51.
Best Maps: ADK Trails of the High Peaks Region. Discover the Adirondack High Peaks.
Access: The Garden to Johns Brook DEC Interior Outpost (3.1 mi.). AMR/Lake Road.
Trails to Summit: ADK Range Trail from DEC Interior Outpost (3.9 mi.). Beaver Meadow Trail from Lake Road to Range Trail (3.4 mi.).
Comments: Armstrong, named for Thomas Armstrong, a landowner, is the next major peak along the Great Range. The climb from Upper Wolf Jaw is very steep in places as it winds around cliffs and ledges to the partially open summit which has spectacular views. Like the Wolf Jaws and Gothics, this peak can be climbed from either the Johns Brook Lodge area (after first climbing either Gothics or Upper Wolfjaw) or from the Adirondack Mountain Reserve lands.

Gothics (38)

Elevation: 4734 ft./1443 m.
USGS Quad/Coordinates: 15' Mt. Marcy: 44N07/73W51.

On the summit of Gothics

Best Maps: ADK Trails of the High Peaks Region. Discover the Adirondack High Peaks.
Access: The Garden to Johns Brook DEC Interior Outpost (3.1 mi.). AMR/Lake Road.
Trails to Summit: Ore Bed Brook Trail from DEC Interior Outpost (3.7 mi.). ADK Range Trail from DEC Interior Outpost (4.8 mi.). Beaver Meadow Trail from Lake Road (3.4 mi.). Alfred E. Weld Trail from Lake Road (2.7 mi.).
Comments: With its slide scars on its steep sides, Gothics is not only visually striking itself, but offers equally striking vistas from its slides and summit. Along the trail on its southern face, which is very steep and open to high winds, a cable has been cemented to the bedrock to assist hikers. A portion of the mountain extends to the east offering an additional views. Beyond this extension is Pyramid, and eastern spur or the mountain, with its outstanding views of the region with a different perspective.

Saddleback Mountain (38)

Elevation: 4528 ft./1380 m.
USGS Quad/Coordinates: 15' Mt. Marcy: 44N07/73W53.
Best Maps: ADK Trails of the High Peaks Region. Discover the Adirondack High Peaks.
Access: The Garden to Johns Brook DEC Interior Outpost (3.1 mi.).
Trail to Summit: Ore Bed Brook Trail to State Range Trail (3.6 mi.).
Comments: There are two humps on this mountain that give it its name. Facing the Gothics/Saddleback col is the lower summit from which there is a view back to Gothics. The higher southern hump has an excellent overlook to the south over a steep and dangerous cliff, down which the Range Trail drops on its way to Basin.

Basin Mountain (38)

Elevation: 4826 ft./1471 m.

USGS Quad/Coordinates: 15' Mt. Marcy: 44N07/73W54.

Best Maps: ADK Trails of the High Peaks Region. Discover the Adirondack High Peaks.

Access: The Garden to Johns Brook DEC Interior Outpost (3.1 mi.).

Trails to Summit: State Range Trail over Saddleback (4.5 mi.). Phelps Trail to Slant Rock, Shorey Short Cut to Range Trail (5.4 mi.).

Comments: The descent from Saddleback and the climb to Basin are steep and challenging. The upper levels of Basin are terraced; the open summit is reached after climbing through several high, level sections.

Mt. Haystack (38)

Elevation: 4961 ft./1512 m.

USGS Quad/Coordinates: 15' Mt. Marcy: 44N06/73W54.

Best Maps: ADK Trails of the High Peaks Region. Discover the Adirondack High Peaks.

Access: The Garden to Johns Brook DEC Interior Outpost (3.1 mi.). Elk Lake.

Trails to Summit: Phelps Trail/State Range Trail/Haystack Trail (5.8 mi.). Orebed Brook Trail/State Range Trail over Saddleback and Basin (6.4 mi.). A southern approach is possible using the Elk Lake-Marcy Trail from Elk Lake to Panther Gorge and then to the very steep Haystack trail (about 10.5 mi.).

Comments: Haystack, the third highest peak in the Adirondacks, is considered by many to have the best view of all. One dramatic feature is the 2,000-ft. drop into Panther Gorge between this mountain and nearby Marcy. A large portion of the summit is above treeline, potentially dangerous in bad weather.

Like its giant neighbors, Marcy and Skylight, Haystack is far from parking areas and thus requires serious trip planning. The shortest distance from The Garden to its summit is about 17 miles round trip.

Marcy and its Neighbors

Mt. Marcy (39)

Elevation: 5344 ft./1629 m.
USGS Quad/Coordinates: 15' Mt. Marcy: 44N07/73W55.
Best Maps: ADK Trails of the High Peaks Region. Discover the Adirondack High Peaks.
Access: The Garden to Johns Brook DEC Interior Outpost (3.1 mi.). Adirondack Loj. Upper Works.
Trails to Summit: Phelps Trail (6 mi. from JBL -- 9.1 from Garden). Hopkins Trail (6.1 mi. from JBL). Hovenberg Trail from Adirondack Loj (7.4 mi.). Calamity Brook Trail (and others) from Upper Works (10.3 mi.), from Lake Colden DEC Interior Outpost (5.2 mi.).
Comments: This, the highest summit in the Adirondacks, was named for William Learned Marcy, a governor of New York. It was first climbed in 1837, nearly 200 years after Mt. Washington was climbed by Darby Field; this is one indication of how long the High Peaks remained a true wilderness. Its summit cone lies well above treeline; because of its #1 rank and its excellent views, it is rarely without hikers or dogs on top. A plaque located on the peak commemorates the centennial of the first climb, an event that brought 500 pounds of radio transmission equipment to its summit.

Vice President Theodore Roosevelt was hiking near Marcy when he received the news that President William McKinley had been shot and was dying. After rushing out of the mountains he was informed that McKinley had died and he had become the next president.

Marcy is often climbed as a long day-hike from Adirondack Loj via the Hovenberg trail; a round trip of about 15 miles. This is the shortest route to the summit. From the Garden, the round trip is over 18 miles; from Upper Works, 21 miles. A one-day approach from these latter trailheads is strenuous, though many do it. Many hikers prefer to camp and then day-hike Marcy and neighboring peaks. It is for this reason that the Johns Brook DEC Interior Outpost is the starting point from which ascents of peaks in the Marcy/Great Range area are measured. The Lake Colden DEC Interior Outpost and vicinity is another possible base for trips to Marcy.

Nearing the summit of Marcy

Gray Peak (39)

Elevation: 4826 ft./1471 m.
USGS Quad/Coordinates: 15' Mt. Marcy: 44N07/73W56.
Best Maps: ADK Trails of the High Peaks Region. Discover the Adirondack High Peaks.
Access: Adirondack Loj. Upper Works. The Garden to Johns Brook DEC Interior Outpost.
Trail to Summit: No official trail. Feldspar Brook Trail to the summit herd path is the usual route.
Comments: This mountain, connected to Marcy, is the highest peak in the Adirondacks without an officially maintained trail to its ridge-like summit. A herd path begins at the outlet of Lake Tear of the Clouds off the Feldspar Brook Trail. In order to reach the summit from Johns Brook DEC Interior Outpost, it is necessary to climb Marcy first. Gray was named for Harvard botanist Asa Gray.

Mt. Skylight (39)

Elevation: 4925 ft./1501 m.
USGS Quad/Coordinates: 15' Mt. Marcy: 44N06/73W56.
Best Maps: ADK Trails of the High Peaks Region. Discover the Adirondack High Peaks.

Access: Adirondack Loj. Upper Works. The Garden to Johns Brook DEC Interior Outpost (3.1 mi.).
Trails to Summit: Skylight trail from Four Corners (0.5 mi.).
Comments: A slightly lesser companion of Haystack and Marcy, Skylight is a giant in itself. Its summit dome contains an extensive alpine area of open rock with excellent views and a large pile of small rocks. A custom has been established by hikers who believe that failing to carry up and deposit a stone on Skylight's summit cairn will insure a rainfall.

The Skylight trail reaches the summit from Four Corners, a junction of trails. Four Corners itself is about 7 miles from either Adirondack Loj or Johns Brook Lodge. A hike from Johns Brook requires a climb of Marcy each way.

Allen Mountain (40)

Elevation: 4347 ft., 1325 m.
USGS Quad/Coordinates: 15' Mt. Marcy: 44N04/73W57.
Best Maps: ADK Trails of the High Peaks Region. Discover the Adirondack High Peaks.
Access: Upper Works.
Trails to Summit: A herd path from former Twin Brooks Lean-to is the usual route.
Comments: Allen is one of the more remote peaks in the Adirondacks and climbing it will require much trip planning. The herd path follows Skylight Brook and then Allen Brook on its way to the wooded summit with limited views. There are a number of waterfalls along Allen Brook that make the hike more interesting. Allen was named for a Boston clergyman who spent summers in Keene Valley.

Skylight from Gray   *Photo by Thomas R. Berrian*

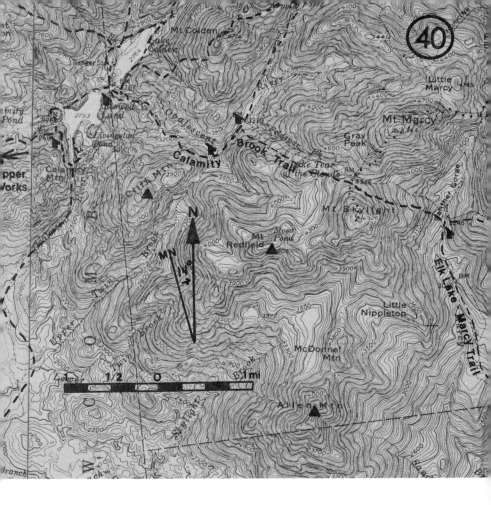

Mt. Redfield (40)

Elevation: 4606 ft./1404 m.

USGS Quad/Coordinates: 15' Mt. Marcy: 44N06/73W57.

Best Maps: ADK Trails of the High Peaks Region. Discover the Adirondack High Peaks.

Access: Adirondack Loj. Upper Works.

Trail to Summit: The usual route is to follow Uphill Brook, then to a tributary on the right which becomes a herd path.

Comments: The great Adirondack surveyor Verplanck Colvin named this peak for William C. Redfield, geologist and meteorologist who was, along with Colvin, an early explorer of the region. The path to the wooded summit has a view to the north and the summit offers a very good view south to Allen, the Dix range and beyond.

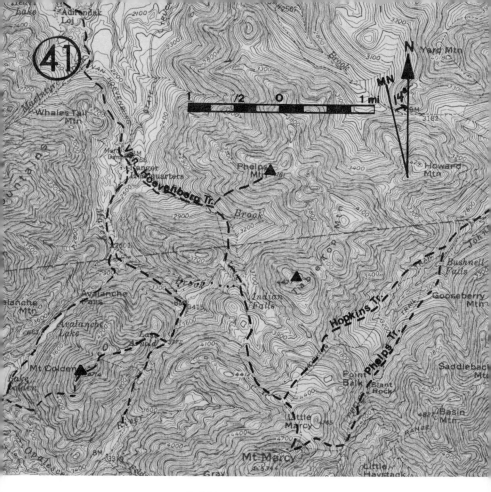

Cliff Mountain (40)

Elevation: 3944 ft./1202 m.

USGS Quad/Coordinates: 15' Mt. Marcy: 44N06/73W58.

Best Maps: ADK Trails of the High Peaks Region. Discover the Adirondack High Peaks.

Access: Adirondack Loj. Upper Works.

Trail to Summit: Herd paths lead to summit from Uphill Brook Lean-to.

Comments: Cliff is named for the steep cliffs on its southeast face that are not apparent to most who climb it. The climb is not particularly difficult, except for the fact that it lies far from any convenient trailhead. It could be difficult and dangerous if one leaves the herd path and descends in the wrong place. Its summit (there are two, the true one is to the south) is wooded but there are limited views from the herd paths on the way. Although Cliff is lower than 4,000 ft., it was once believed to have been over that benchmark and thus became one of the sacred 46.

Phelps Mountain (41)

Elevation: 4160 ft./1268 m.
USGS Quad/Coordinates: 15' Mt. Marcy: 44N09/73W55.
Best Maps: ADK Trails of the High Peaks Region. Discover the Adirondack High Peaks.
Access: Adirondack Loj.
Trail to Summit: Phelps Trail via Van Hoevenberg Trail (4.4 mi.).
Comments: This peak was named for the most famous Adirondack guide of them all, Orson Schofield "Old Mountain" Phelps, one of the great characters of Adirondack history. The trail begins about 3 miles from Adirondack Loj and reaches the open summit ledges in just over a mile.

Table Top Mountain (41)

Elevation: 4413 ft./1345 m.
USGS Quad/Coordinates: 15' Mt. Marcy: 44N08/73W55.
Best Maps: ADK Trails of the High Peaks Region. Discover the Adirondack High Peaks.
Access: Adirondack Loj. The Garden to Johns Brook DEC Interior Outpost (3.1 mi.).
Trail to Summit: Herd path.
Comments: Herd paths to the wooded summit start near Indian Falls on the Hoevenberg Trail. Climbing this peak, as well as any of the others without officially maintained trails, requires careful trip planning and exercising path-finding skills. South of the summit are some lookouts. Although Table Top looks flat-topped from other peaks, it has two lower summits, one of which would count as a 4000-footer under AMC rules.

Mt. Colden (41)

Elevation: 4715 ft./1437 m.
USGS Quad/Coordinates: 15' Mt. Marcy: 44N07/73W57.
Best Maps: ADK Trails of the High Peaks Region. Discover the Adirondack High Peaks.
Access: Adirondack Loj.
Trails to Summit: From Lake Colden (1.6 mi./7.4 mi. from Adirondack Loj). From Lake Arnold (1.4 mi./6.3 mi. from Adirondack Loj).
Comments: The slides on the western side of the mountain are

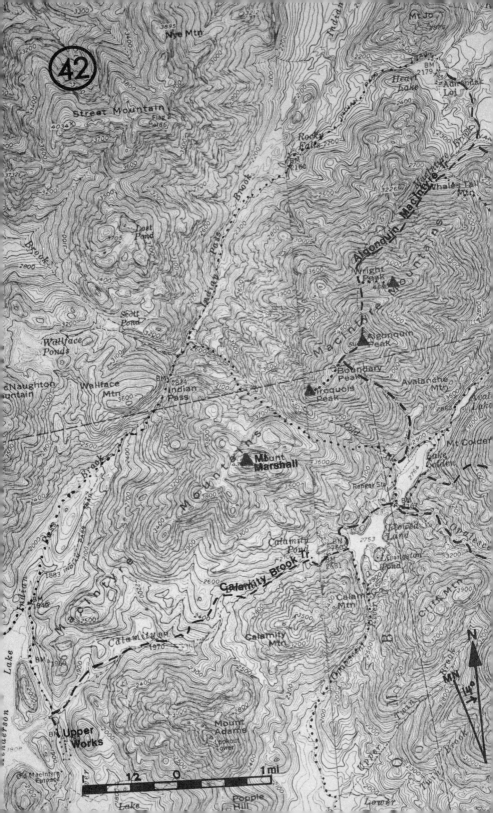

Colden and Marcy (background) from Algonquin

particularly dramatic and are also used as a route to the summit. The climb from Lake Colden is steeper than that from Lake Arnold. The actual summit is an exposed alpine environment with views toward Algonquin which is due west. A lower northern extension of the summit offers more of the same. Colden was named for a New York socialite who was involved in the establishment of the iron mines and did some early exploration of the region.

MacIntyre Range

Wright Peak (42)

Elevation: 4587 ft./1398 m.
USGS Quad/Coordinates: 15' Mt. Marcy: 44N09/73W59.
Best Maps: ADK Trails of the High Peaks Region. Discover the Adirondack High Peaks.
Access: Adirondack Loj.
Trail to Summit: Via Algonquin/MacIntyre trail (3.5 mi.).
Comments: Wright Peak was named for NY governor Silas Wright. Its summit is rocky and above treeline (an alpine zone) and therefore quite fragile. Please stay on the rocks and the marked path. The summit is reached via a steep side trail east of the Algonquin/MacIntyre Trail which traverses the northern part of the MacIntyre Range.

Algonquin Peak (42)

Elevation: 5115 ft./1559 m.
USGS Quad/Coordinates: 15' Mt. Marcy: 44N08/73W59.
Best Maps: ADK Trails of the High Peaks Region. Discover the Adirondack High Peaks.
Access: Adirondack Loj.
Trails to Summit: Algonquin/MacIntyre trail (4 mi.). Via Lake Colden (5 mi.).
Comments: Algonquin Peak is the highest summit of the MacIntyre Range and the second highest peak in the Adirondacks. It is well above treeline and supports a community of fragile alpine plants -- please stay on the marked route. The accessibility of this peak, only 4 miles from Adirondack Loj, has made it very popular with hikers and not often a place for solitude. Algonquin offers many dramatic views including Colden's immense slide scars and, behind Colden, Mt. Marcy's towering summit cone.

Iroquois Peak (42)

Elevation: 4849 ft./1478 m. **USGS Quad/Coordinates:** 15' Mt. Marcy: 44N08/74W00.
Best Maps: ADK Trails of the High Peaks Region. Discover the Adirondack High Peaks.
Access: Adirondack Loj.
Trail to Summit: Herd path.
Comments: This high summit along the MacIntyre Range is reached via a well-used herd path that first passes over Boundary Peak then climbs Iroquois. This path begins where the MacIntyre/Algonquin trail turns sharply east in the col between Algonquin and Boundary Peak. The narrow summit ridge is wide open and offers excellent views toward the west and the Santanoni range. Algonquin and Iroquois were named for the two Native American peoples whose territories extended into the Adirondacks.

Mt. Marshall (42)

Elevation: 4379 ft./1330+ m.
USGS Quad/Coordinates: 15' Santanoni, 15' Mt. Marcy: 44N08/74W01.

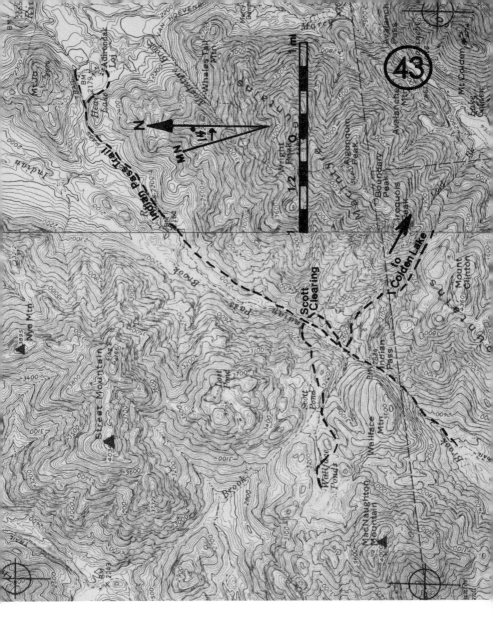

Best Maps: ADK Trails of the High Peaks Region. Discover the
Adirondack High Peaks.

Access: Upper Works. Adirondack Loj.

Trail to Summit: Herd path.

Comments: Named for Robert Marshall, who (with his brother George
and Herbert Clark) established the tradition of climbing the 46 peaks
thought to be over 4,000 ft. in the 1920's. Bob Marshall went on to become

a well-known explorer, the founder of the Wilderness Society, and a leader in forestry matters. It is the southernmost peak in the MacIntyre Range and it is reachable only via herd paths. Although its summit is wooded, lookouts do exist.

West of the MacIntyre Range

Nye Mountain (43)

Elevation: 3887 ft./1180+ m.
USGS Quad/Coordinates: 15' Santanoni, 15' Mt. Marcy: 44N12/74W02.
Best Maps: ADK Trails of the High Peaks Region. Discover the Adirondack High Peaks.
Access: Adirondack Loj.
Trail to Summit: Herd path.
Comments: Nye and nearby Street are challenging climbs because there are no official trails and because large areas of blowdowns inhibit progress. Nye, in particular, can be confusing. It was named for Verplanck Colvin's guide, William B. Nye. Its summit, it has been said, sets the standard for wooded summits. Like Blake, Cliff and Couchsachraga, an early survey measured it at over 4,000 ft. and so it entered the list of the Adirondack Forty-Sixers.

Street Mountain (43)

Elevation: 4150 ft./1260+ m.
USGS Quad/Coordinates: 15' Santanoni, 15' Mt. Marcy: 44N11/74W03.
Best Maps: ADK Trails of the High Peaks Region. Discover the Adirondack High Peaks. **Access:** Adirondack Loj.
Trails to Summit: Herd path.
Comments: This mountain was named for Alfred B. Street, a librarian and writer who journeyed through the Adirondacks in the 1860's. Although the summit is wooded, there is a good lookout. Street is usually climbed on the same trip as Nye by hikers seeking to join the Forty Sixers. As mentioned under Nye, the going can be difficult and such a trip requires planning and experience.

MacNaughton Mountain (43)

Elevation: 3983 ft./1214 m.
USGS Quad/Coordinates: 15' Santanoni, 15' Mt. Marcy: 44N08/74W04.
Best Maps: ADK Trails of the High Peaks Region. Discover the Adirondack High Peaks.
Access: Upper Works. Adirondack Loj.
Trail to Summit: Herd path.
Comments: Originally thought to be under 4,000 feet, the 1953 survey raised it to exactly that figure. The current survey lowered it again. MacNaughton is not required by the Adirondack Forty Sixers, though many who aspire to that goal do climb it. (It is still higher than Blake, Cliff, Nye and Couchsachraga). The mountain was named for James MacNaughton, a descendant of Archibald MacIntyre, who ran the Adirondack Iron Works.

Santanoni Mountains

Panther Peak (44)

Elevation: 4442 ft./1354 m.
USGS Quad/Coordinates: 15' Santanoni: 44N06/74W08.
Best Maps: Discover the Adirondack High Peaks. ADK Trails of the High Peaks Region.
Access: Upper Works to near Bradley Pond Lean-to. Note: Trail to Bradley Pond is over private land. Respect boundaries.
Trail to Summit: Herd path from north of Bradley Pond.
Comments: Panther is usually climbed along with Santanoni and Couchsachraga by aspiring Forty-Sixers. The route from near Bradley Pond Lean-to heads straight for Couchsachraga; the route between the summits of Panther and Santanoni crosses this at a right angle, this intersection being known as "Times Square." The summit of Panther has good views to the west.

Santanoni Peak (44)

Elevation: 4606 ft./1404 m.
USGS Quad/Coordinates: 15' Santanoni: 44N05/74W08.

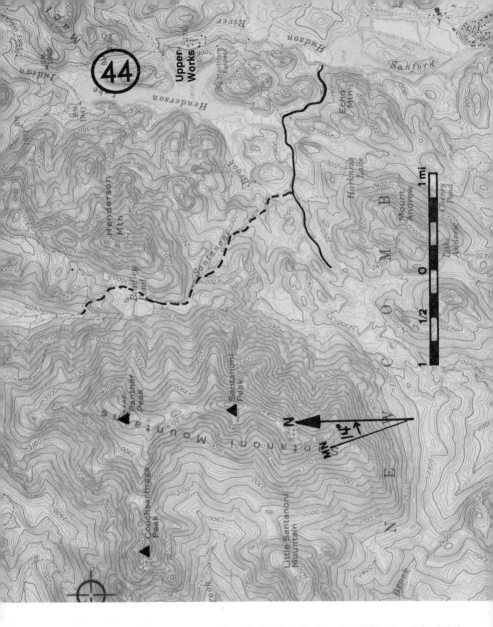

Best Maps: Discover the Adirondack High Peaks. ADK Trails of the High Peaks Region.

Access: Upper works to near Bradley Pond Lean-to. Note: Trail to Bradley Pond is over private land. Respect boundaries.

Trail to Summit: Herd path from north of Bradley Pond.

Comments: See description for Panther. The herd path from Times Square follows the long Panther/Santanoni ridge, eventually reaching the summit. There are excellent views from an overlook nearby. The name

Santanoni is probably a corruption of Saint Anthony, but it is not clear how it received that name.

Couchsachraga Peak (44)

Elevation: 3793 ft./1156 m.
USGS Quad/Coordinates: 15' Santanoni: 44N06/74W10.
Best Maps: Discover the Adirondack High Peaks. ADK Trails of the High Peaks Region.
Access: Upper Works to near Bradley Pond Lean-to. Note: Trail to Bradley Pond is over private land. Respect boundaries.
Trail to Summit: Herd path north of Bradley Pond.
Comments: This mountain, considerably lower than the limit used in this book, was originally thought to have measured over 4,000 feet and hence became one of the original 46 peaks of the Forty Sixers. In fact, modern surveys indicate that there are 15 other non-Forty-Sixer mountains higher than this one. The name, an Iroquois word, means "dismal wilderness."

Santanoni Range from Street   *Photo by E.C.Hudowalski, courtesy ADK*

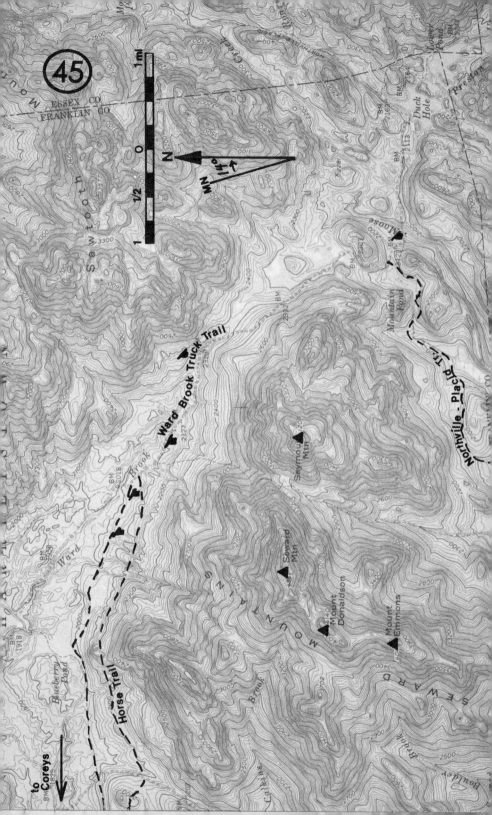

The mountain, usually climbed on the same trip with Panther and Santanoni, is remote and presents challenges. There are views from one of two wooded summits.

The Seward Mountains

Seymour Mountain (45)

Elevation: 4091 ft./1247 m.
USGS Quad/Coordinates: 15' Santanoni: 44N10/74W10.
Best Maps: Discover the Adirondack High Peaks. ADK Trails of the High Peaks Region.
Access: Coreys Road.
Trail to Summit: Herd path.
Comments: Named for a NY governor, Horatio Seymour, this mountain's summit has good views of the entire Seward Range. The herd path to the summit utilizes part of a slide.

Seward Mountain (45)

Elevation: 4347 ft./1320+ m.
USGS Quad/Coordinates: 15' Santanoni: 44N10/74W12.
Best Maps: Discover the Adirondack High Peaks. ADK Trails of the High Peaks Region.
Access: Coreys Road.
Trail to Summit: Herd path.
Comments: This mountain is named for yet another NY governor, William Henry Seward. There are views just south of the wooded summit.

Mount Donaldson (45)

Elevation: 4108 ft./1252 m.
USGS Quad/Coordinates: 15' Santanoni: 44N09/74W13.
Best Maps: Discover the Adirondack High Peaks. ADK Trails of the High Peaks Region **Access:** Coreys Road.
Trail to Summit: Herd path.

Comments: Named for a writer on the history of the Adirondacks, Donaldson is usually reached after climbing Seward. The summit offers good views to the east.

Mount Emmons (45)

Elevation: 4039 ft./1231 m.
USGS Quad/Coordinates: 15' Santanoni: 44N09/74W13.
Best Maps: Discover the Adirondack High Peaks. ADK Trails of the High Peaks Region.
Access: Coreys Road.
Trail to Summit: Herd path.
Comments: This mountain was named for geologist Ebenezer Emmons who led the first recorded climb of Mt. Marcy in 1837. The summit is

The cannister on Cliff

Chapter 6

The Catskill Mountains of New York State

Geology of the Catskills

The Catskill mountains are of an entirely different nature than the other high ranges of the Northeast. They are a deeply eroded plateau of sedimentary rock, not a buckled and contorted range like the Green Mountains nor granite intrusions like the Whites. Visible proof of this is found from any high summit or overlook; the tops of the peaks are nearly all of the same height. The dense vegetation keeps the Catskills from resembling the eroded canyons and mesas of the American Southwest. Without the tree cover, the relief would be sharper and the landforms more bizarre. The distance from valleys to summits in the Catskills is considerable, 2,000 feet or more in places; if bare and dry, this vertical rise would translate into some very dramatic rock scenery, in some ways resembling the Superstition Wilderness of Arizona. But the Northeast is a well-watered place and hikers must scale the summits to the many perches of ledge to see this terrain for what it is.

The rock of the Catskills is sedimentary, mostly shales and sandstones that were deposited about 400 million years ago under a vast inland sea that extended throughout the interior of the continent. These deposits of mud and sand originated from the erosion of a range of high mountains to the east, a range that no longer exists. Later, this sea floor was uplifted and became the Allegheny Plateau, of which the Catskills and Pennsylvania's Pocono Mountains are a part. The uplift in the Catskill region was high, perhaps as much as five or six thousand feet. Wind, water and ice did their work to reduce the elevation and carve the region into its present shape. Glaciation also affected the present scenery, scraping topsoil off summits and rounding out valleys, but this activity was much less intense than in the other ranges to the north.

Hiking Clubs in the Catskills

The **New York-New Jersey Trail Conference** began in 1920 as an umbrella group for the local hiking clubs of the region. This organization publishes the *New York Walk Book* which contains a section on the Catskills. They also publish *Hiking the Catskills*, a guidebook to the area, and the best maps of the region which are printed in four colors on quality waterproof and tearproof paper. The Trail Conference has long been active in the Catskills and maintains many trails there.

The **Catskill 3500 Club** was organized in 1962 to promote climbs on peaks over 3,500 feet. They publish the quarterly *Catskill Canister* which lists their activities and news items. To be a member one must complete climbs of the 35 peaks on the list, four of them to be done two times, once in winter. Although the elevations of the peaks aren't all that high, one should consider that 16 of them are trailless; they have no marked trails to their summits. A listing of these peaks is at the end of this section.

Some chapters of the **Adirondack Mountain Club (ADK)** are also active in the Catskills. See the description under the section on Adirondack Hiking Clubs. ADK also publishes a Catskill guidebook, *Guide to Catskill Trails.*

Land Ownership and Management in the Catskills

The Catskill Mountains are protected as a forest preserve within the boundaries of The Catskill Park, established in 1894 by the State Forest Preserve Act. The New York Department of Conservation (DEC) maintains and protects the state land in the Catskills.

Hiking Trails in the Catskills

Since the New York DEC also manages the Adirondacks, there are some similarities between trail systems in the two regions. A number of Adirondack-style leantos exist in the Catskills, usually located well below the summits. Camping is not allowed over 3500 ft. Most trails are well-maintained and marked with metal discs. The Long Path, a blue-blazed trail that begins near New York City, crosses the heart of the Catskills and traverses a number of major peaks. Hikers should note that water is scarce at high elevations in the Catskills.

On the summit of Slide Mountain

New York's Catskill Mountains

Mountain	Elevation:feet/m	Date(s) Climbed
1. Slide	4180/1274	_____
2. Hunter	4040/1231	_____
3. Black Dome	3980/1213	_____
4. Blackhead	3940/1201	_____
5. Thomas Cole	3940/1201	_____

DIRECTORY OF CATSKILL MOUNTAIN SUMMITS

The Blackhead Range

Blackhead (46)

Elevation: 3940 ft./1201 m.
USGS Quad/Coordinates: 7.5'Freehold, 7.5' Hensonville: 42N16/74W06.
Best Maps: NY/NJ Trail Conference #41: Northeast Catskills.
Access: Maplecrest: county road #56 (Big Hollow Road).
Trail to Summit: Black Dome Range Trail to Blackhead Mountain Trail (2.3 mi.).
Comments: Blackhead is the easternmost summit on the Blackhead Range. It can be easily day-hiked from the state parking area at the head of the Black Dome Valley. There is a lookout to the southwest on the summit.

Black Dome (46)

Elevation: 3980 ft./1213 m.
USGS Quad/Coordinates: 7.5' Freehold, 7.5' Hensonville: 42N16/74W07.
Best Maps: NY/NJ Trail Conference #41: Northeast Catskills.
Access: Maplecrest: county road #56 (Big Hollow Road).

Trail to Summit: Black Dome Range Trail (2.3 mi.).
Comments: This is the middle mountain of the Blackhead Range, an east-west range in the northern Catskills. The Black Dome Range Trail crosses all three summits and can be hiked in one day if a car shuttle is arranged. Its summit, like all high Catskill summits, is a northern forest of spruce and fir. There is a ledge near the summit with views to the south. Ledges on the trail heading down and north of this peak offer even better views.

Thomas Cole (46)

Elevation: 3940 ft./1201 m.
USGS Quad/Coordinates: 7.5' Hensonville, 7.5' Freehold: 42N16/74W08.
Best Maps: NY/NJ Trail Conference #41: Northeast Catskills.
Access: Maplecrest: county road #40 (Maplecrest Road) to Elmer Barnum Road, or county road #56 (Big Hollow Road).
Trail to Summit: Black Dome Range Trail: from Elmer Barnum Road (2.9 mi.), from Big Hollow Road over Black Dome (3.1 mi.).
Comments: Named for the famed Hudson River School painter, this mountain is the western peak of the Blackhead Range. There is a southward looking vista at the summit which is in the spruce/fir zone.

Descending between Blackhead and Black Dome

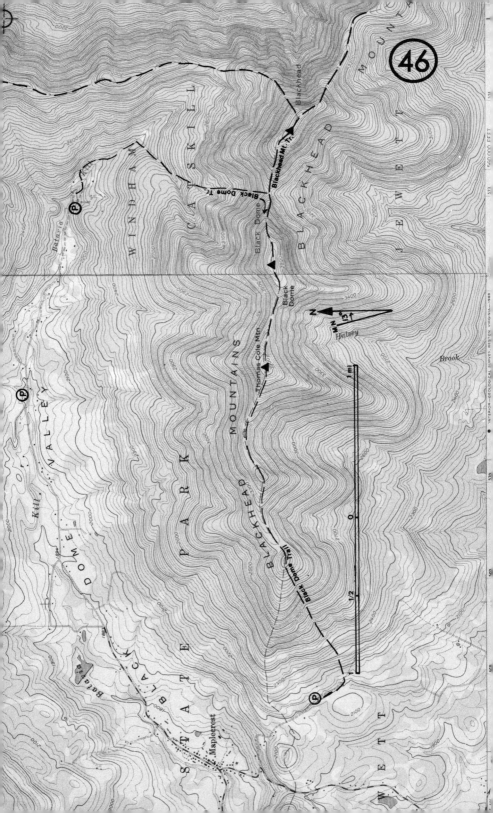

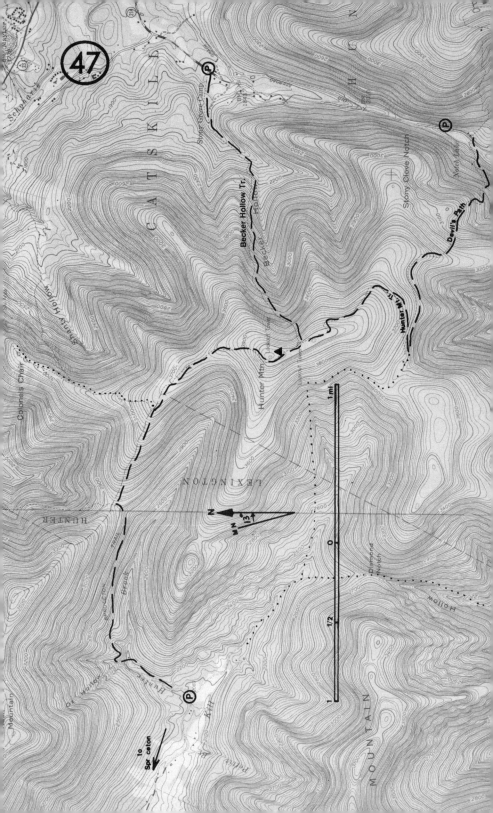

Other Catskill Peaks: The 4,000 footers

Hunter Mountain (47)

Elevation: 4040 ft./1231 m.
USGS Quad/Coordinates: 7.5' Hunter, 7.5' Lexington: 42N11/74W14.
Best Maps: NY/NJ Trail Conference #41: Northeast Catskills.
Access: Hunter: NY 214, Spruceton: county road #6.
Trail to Summit: Becker Hollow Trail to Spruceton Trail (2.6 mi.).
Devil's Path to Hunter Mountain to Becker Hollow/Spruceton trails (3.3 mi.).
Comments: Hunter is a massive mountain that supports a large ski area as well as several hiking trails. The summit is flat and covered with spruce and fir, but a state fire tower is located on it from which there are excellent views.

Slide Mountain (48)

Elevation: 4180 ft./1274 m.
USGS Quad/Coordinates: 7.5' Peekamoose Mtn., 7.5' Shandaken, 7.5' West Shokan: 42N00/74W23.
Best Maps: NY/NJ Trail Conference #43: Southern Catskills.
Access: Woodland Valley State Campground. Oliverea-Big Indian Road/Slide Mountain Road (#47) near Winnisook Lake. Denning. **Trails to Summit:** Wittenberg-Cornell-Slide Trail (7 mi.). Phoenicia East Branch Trail from Rt. 47 to Wittenberg-Cornell-Slide Trail (2.7 mi.). Phoenicia-East Branch Trail from Denning to Curtis-Ormsbee Trail to Wittenberg-Cornell-Slide Trail (5.3 mi.).
Comments: Slide is the highest peak in the Catskills and it attracts many hikers. The easiest way up is from Rt. 47 near Winnisook Lake, but this route is not particularly scenic. The most challenging is the Wittenberg-Cornell-Slide Trail, requiring climbs of the other two before Slide is taken on. The summit has a clearing and excellent views. There is a plaque on the summit in memory of naturalist John Burroughs, who climbed Slide frequently.

Catskill 3500 Club Summits

Mountain	Elevation: ft/m	Date(s) climbed
1. Slide*	4180/1274	_____
2. Hunter	4040/1231	_____
3. Black Dome	3980/1213	_____
4. Thomas Cole	3940/1201	_____
5. Blackhead*	3940/1201	_____
6. Westkill	3880/1183	_____
7. Graham	3868/1180	_____
8. Doubletop#	3860/1177	_____
9. Cornell	3860/1177	_____
10. Table	3847/1173	_____
11. Peekamoose	3843/1171	_____
12. Plateau	3840/1170	_____
13. Sugarloaf	3800/1158	_____
14. Wittenberg	3780/1152	_____
15. Southwest Hunter#	3740/1140	_____
16. Lone#	3721/1134	_____
17. Balsam Lake	3720/1134	_____
18. Panther*	3720/1134	_____
19. Big Indian#	3700/1128	_____
20. Friday#	3694/1126	_____
21. Rusk#	3680/1122	_____
22. High Peak	3655/1114	_____
23. Twin	3640/1109	_____
24. Balsam Cap#	3623/1104	_____
25. Fir#	3620/1103	_____
26. North Dome#	3610/1100	_____
27. Eagle	3600/1097	_____
28. Balsam*	3600/1097	_____
29. Bearpen	3600/1097	_____
30. Indian Head	3573/1089	_____
31. Sherrill#	3540/1079	_____
32. Vly#	3529/1076	_____
33. Windham High Peak	3524/1074	_____
34. Halcott#	3520/1073	_____
35. Rocky#	3508/1069	_____

Must be climbed twice; at least once in winter plus any other season.
 # Trailless summits.

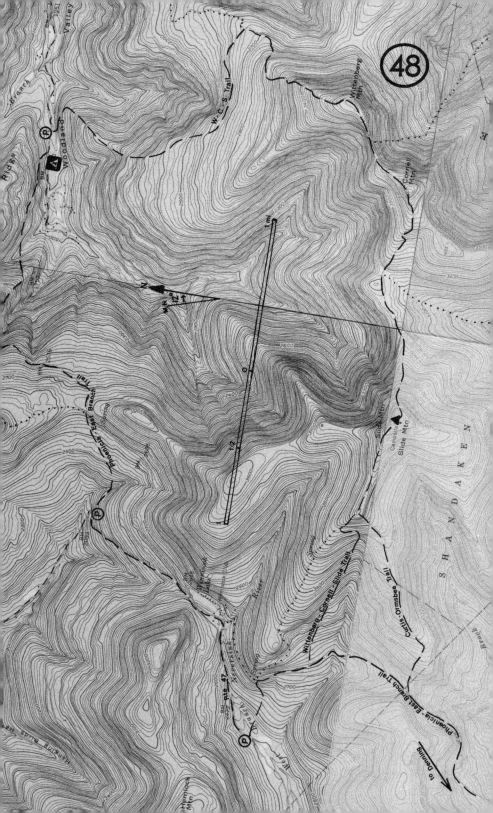

Chapter 7

Sources for Guides, Books, Maps and Clubs

Guidebooks

Maine

Appalachian Mountain Club. *AMC Maine Mountain Guide.* Boston: Appalachian Mountain Club. 1988.
(A good source of information on Maine's mountains, including the higher peaks. Comes with AMC maps of Katahdin and the Rangeley- Stratton area.)

Caputo, Cloe. *Fifty Hikes in Northern Maine.* Woodstock, VT: Backcountry Publications. 1989.

Clark, Stephen. *Katahdin: A Guide to Baxter State Park and Katahdin.* Unity, ME: North Country Press. 1985.

Maine Appalachian Trail Club. *Guide to the Applachian Trail in Maine.* Augusta, ME: Maine Applachian Trail Club. 1988.
(Since the Appalachian Trail traverses nearly all of Maine's highest summits, this guide, which comes with a set of excellent maps, may prove of value to those exploring the region.)

New Hampshire

Appalachian Mountain Club. *AMC White Mountain Guide.* Boston: Appalachian Mountain Club. 1992.
(This is the established guidebook of the White Mountains. It includes specific trail information, directions, current rules and regualtions, etc. Separate maps of all parts of the White Mountains are included.)

Doan, Daniel. *Fifty Hikes in the White Mountains.* Woodstock, VT: Backcountry Publications. 1973, 1990.

Doan, Daniel. *Fifty More Hikes in New Hamshire.* Woodstock, VT: Backcountry Publications. 1978, 1991.

Preston, Philip and Jonathan A. Kannair. *White Mountains WEST.* Ashland, New Hampshire: Waumbek Books. 1979. (This is an excellent guide to the central and western region of the White Mountains. Much technical data on trails and summits is presented along with portions of Preston's excellent map. Although some trail information is dated, the book comes with attached updates. Order from Waumbek Books, Box 573, Ashland, NH 03217.)

Vermont

Green Mountain Club. *Fifty Hikes in Vermont.* Woodstock, VT: Backcountry Publications. 1990.

Green Mountain Club. *Guide Book of the Long Trail.* Waterbury Center, VT: Green Mountain Club. 1990.
(Since all of the high peaks in Vermont are traversed by the Long Trail, this is the book to own.)

New York: Adirondacks

Adirondack Mountain Club. *Guide to Adirondack Trails: High Peaks Region.* Lake George, NY: Adirondack Mountain Club. 1992.
(Of the 8 guidebooks to the Adirondacks published by ADK (Adirondack Mountain Club), this is the one that contains data on the highest summits. If you hike and climb in the Adirondacks, this guide is a must.

McMartin, Barbara. *Discover the Adirondack High Peaks.* Woodstock, VT: Backcountry Publications. 1989. (Includes a good map that is also available separately on Tyvek. This book is invaluable for those seeking to climb the trailless peaks. McMartin has also authored several other books on other sections of the Adirondacks, published by Backcountry Publications.)

New York: Catskills

McAllister, Lee and Myron Steven Ochman. *Hiking The Catskills.* New York: NY/NJ Trail Conference. 1989.
(A good guide and record of personal experiences on the Catskill peaks, including those that are trailless.)

McMartin, Barbara, and Peter Kick. *Fifty Hikes in the Hudson Valley.* Woodstock, VT: Backcountry Publications. 1985.

Wadsworth, Bruce, and the Schenectady Chapter of ADK. *Guide to Catskill Trails.* Lake George, NY: Adirondack Mountain Club. 1988.

Publications on Geology

Jaffe, Elizabeth B. and Howard W. *Geology of the Adirondack High Peaks Region.* Lake George, NY: Adirondack Mountain Club. 1986.

Jorgensen, Neil. *A Guide to New England's Landscape.* Chester, CT: Pequot Press. 1977.

Kendall, David L. *Glaciers & Granite: A Guide to Maine's Landscape and Geology.* Camden, ME: Down East Books, 1987.

Ogburn Jr., Charlton. *The Forging of Our Continent.* New York: American Heritage Publishing Co. 1968.

Raymo, Chet and Maureen E. Raymo. *Written in Stone: A Geological and Natural History of the Northeastern United States.* Chester, CT: The Globe Pequot Press. 1989.

Randall, Peter E., editor. *New Hampshire's Land.* Hanover, NH: Profiles Publishing Corp. 1976.

Van Diver, Bradford B. *Roadside Geology of Vermont and New Hampshire.* Mountain Press Publishing Company, Missoula, MT. 1987.

Wyckoff, Jerome. *The Adirondack Landscape.* Glens Falls, NY: Adirondack Mountain Club. 1967.

Natural History

Marchand, Peter J. *North Woods: An Inside Look at the Nature of Forests in the Northeast.* Boston: Appalachian Mountain Club. 1987.

Steele, Frederic L. *At Timberline: A Nature Guide to the Mountains of the Northeast.* Boston: Applachian Mountain Club.

Sutton, Ann and Myron. *Eastern Forests* (Audubon Society Nature Guides). New York: Alfred A. Knopf. 1992.

History and Personal Experience

Adirondack Forty-Sixers. *Of the Summits, of the Forests.* Morrisonville, NY: Adirondack Forty-Sixers. 1991.
(This is an interesting collection of stories and facts about the Adirondack High Peaks and the Forty-Sixers themselves.)

Belcher, C. Francis. *Logging Railroads of the White Mountains.* Boston: Appalachian Mountain Club.

Carson, Russell M.L., *Peaks and People of the Adirondacks.* Glens Falls, NY: Adirondack Mountain Club. 1927,1986.

Jamieson, Paul, ed. *The Adirondack Reader.* Lake George, NY: Adirondack Mountain Club. 1982.

Morse, Stearns, ed. *Lucy Crawford's History of the White Mountains.* Boston: Appalachian Mountain Club. 1978.

Reifsnyder, William E. *High Huts of the White Mountains*. Boston: Appalachian Mountain Club. 1993.

Underhill, Miriam. *Give Me The Hills*. Riverside, CT: The Chatham Press. 1971.

Waterman, Laura and Guy.*Backwoods Ethics*. Backcountry Press. revised edition. 1993.

Waterman, Laura and Guy. *Wilderness Ethics*. Backcountry Press. 1993.

Waterman, Laura and Guy. *Forest and Crag. A History of Hiking, Trail Blazing, and Adventure in the Northeast Mountains*. Boston: Appalachian Mountain Club. 1989. (Highly recommended work on the mountains and mountaineers of the Northeast. A classic and major reference for years to come.)

Books on Hiking and Backpacking

Angier, Bradford. *How to Stay Alive in the Woods*. New York: Collier Books. 1956.

Dunn, John M. Winterwise: *A Backpacker's Guide*. Lake George, NY: Adirondack Mountain Club.

Fletcher, Colin. *The Complete Walker III*. New York: Alfred A. Knopf. 1992 (revised).

Gorman, Stephen. *AMC Guide to Winter Camping*. Boston: Appalachian Mountain Club. 1991.

Hart, John. *Walking Softly in the Wilderness*. The Sierra Club Guide to Backpacking. San Francisco, CA: Sierra Club Books. 1984.

Isaac, Jeff, PA-C, and Peter Goth, MD. *The Outward Bound Wilderness First-Aid Handbook*. New York: Lyons and Burford. 1991.

Meyer, Kathleen. *How to Shit in the Woods*. Berkely, CA: Ten Speed Press. 1989.

Wilkerson, MD., James, ed. *Medicine for Mountaineering and other Wilderness Activities.* Seattle WA: The Mountaineers. 1992

Maps

Here are the sources for those maps listed in the directories (1993 prices). Write or call ahead for current prices and availability. These sources may also offer other maps of interest. Ask for catalog or price list.

Maine

AMC Baxter Park-Katahdin/Camden Hills/Pleasant Mountain.
This map covers the Katahdin area in detail. In comes in paper (flimsy) for $2.95 or Tyvek (much better) for $4.95.

AMC Carter-Mahoosuc/Rangely-Stratton.
Covers the 4,000-footer section of the Appalachian Trail from Bigelow to Stratton. Unfortunately, it comes only on paper.

Order above maps from Appalachian Mountain Club, PO Box 298 - Mail Order, Gorham, NH 03581. 1-800-262-4455 (orders only).

Map and Guide to the Appalachian Trail in Maine. A set of 7 maps comes with the Appalachian Trail Guide to Maine. Maps 1, 6 and 7 cover sections with high summits. These are good quality maps with shaded contours and an elevation profile. Side trails from the Appalachian Trail are shown. Order the guide and maps from The Main Appalachian Trail Club, Inc. Box 283, Augusta, ME 04330 or from The Appalachian Trail Conference, Inc. PO Box 236, Harpers Ferry, WV 25425.

DeLorme's Map and Guide to Baxter State Park and Katahdin. DeLorme Mapping Company, PO Box 298, Freeport, ME 04032. DeLorme also publishes an excellent atlas to the state of Maine useful when driving to trailheads.

Baxter State Park Map by Stephen Clark. This map comes with Clark's guide to Katahdin (see above).

New Hampshire - White Mountains

AMC 7:Carter-Mahoosuc, 6: Mount Washington, 5: Franconia, 6: Pilot, 4: Chocorua-Waterville. Paper or Tyvek. Order Maps from Appalachian Mountain Club, PO Box 298 - Mail Order, Gorham, NH 08531. 1-800/262-4455 (orders only).

Washington and Lafayette Trail Map. Compiled and drafted by Phillip Preston. Waumbek Books, Box 573, Ashland, NH 03217. This is an excellent map, preferred by many White Mountain hikers. Waumbek Books also publishes a White Mountain Guidebook (see above).

DeLorme's Trail Map and Guide to the White Mountain National Forest. DeLorme Mapping Company. PO Box 298, Freeport ME 04032. DeLorme's state atlas is recommended for locating trailheads.

Trail Map and Guide to the Sandwich Range Wilderness. Wonalancet Out Door Club. Wonalancet, NH 03897. This weather and tear resistant map covers the southern White Mountains from Sandwich Dome to Chocorua. ($5.00 postpaid in 1991).

Vermont - Green Mountains

End to End: Topographic Maps of Vermont's Long Trail. A set of 21 maps, colored and weather resistant. Excellent, affordable and highly recommended.

Order from The Green Mountain Club, address below. Also available from GMC are separate maps of Camel's Hump and Mt. Mansfield.

New York - Adirondacks

Trails of the Adirondack High Peaks Region. An excellent, highly detailed and colored topographic map of the entire High Peaks region. It comes with the purchase of the *Guide to Adirondack Trails: High Peaks Region*, but can be purchased separately or $5.95. Order from the ADK, address above.

Discover the Adirondack High Peaks. A very useful topographic map of the High Peak region that comes with the book *Discover the Adirondack*

High Peaks by Barbara McMartin. It can also be purchased separately in paper ($3.95) or weather resistant paper ($6.95) from Backcountry Publications. PO Box 175, Woodstock, VT 05091. 802/457-1049.

The Adirondack High Peak Region. Plinth, Quoin and Cornice Associates. Bernard R. Miller. Keene Valley, NY 12943. (A large, unwieldy map that covers much territory. Has elevation profiles. Excellent for hanging on a wall.

New York - Catskills

Catskill Trails. A five map set of excellent color topographic maps printed on tough weather-resistant paper. Other maps should be this good. Cost is $12.95 postpaid. Order from The New York- New Jersey Trail Conference, 232 Madison Avenue, NYC 10016.

Sources for USGS Topographic Maps

New England Cartographics
PO Box 9369
North Amherst, MA 01059
413/549-4124

Earth Science Information Center
102-D Hasbrouck Lab
University of Massachusetts
Amherst, MA 01003   413/545-0359

United States Geological Survey
Box 23286, Federal Center, Bldg. 41
Denver, CO 80223

Clubs and Organizations

Adirondack Mountain Club (ADK)
RR 3, Box 3055
Lake George, NY 12845-9523
518/668-4447

Appalachian Mountain Club (AMC)

Randolph Mountain Club
Randolph, NH 03570

Wonalancet Out Door Club
Wonalancet, NH 03897

5 Joy Street
Boston, MA 02108
617/523-0636

Appalachian Trail Conference (ATC)
PO Box 807
Harper's Ferry, WV 25425
304/535-6331

ATC Regional Office in New Hampshire
One Lyme Common
PO Box 312
Lyme, NH 03768

The Green Mountain Club, Inc. (GMC)
RR 1, Box 650, Route 100
Waterbury Center, VT 05677
802/244-7037

NY-NJ Trail Conference (NY/NJTC)
GPO Box 2250
New York, NY 10116
212/685-9699

Peakbagging Clubs or Committees

Adirondack Forty-Sixers, Inc.
R.R. 1, Box 390
Morrisonville, NY 12962-9732

Catskill 3500 Club
41 Morely Avenue
Wyckoff, NJ 07481

AMC Four Thousand Footer Committee
42 Eastman Street
Concord, NH 03301
(This group is the source of the unpublished *Routes to New England Hundred Highest Peaks* which contains the latest information on the more remote, trailless peaks. Send SASE for current price).

The 111ers of Northeastern USA
329 Village Street
Medway, MA 02053

Index of Peaks in order of Elevation

Mountain	State	Elevation: ft./m	Date(s)Climbed
1. Washington	NH	6288/1917	_____
2. Adams	NH	5774/1760	_____
3. Jefferson	NH	5712/1741	_____
4. Monroe	NH	5383/1641*	_____
5. Madison	NH	5367/1636	_____
6. Marcy	NY	5344/1629	_____
7. Katahdin/Baxter	ME	5267/1605	_____
8. Lafayette	NH	5260/1603*	_____
9. Algonquin	NY	5115/1559	_____
10. Lincoln	NH	5089/1551	_____
11. Haystack	NY	4961/1512	_____
12. Skylight	NY	4925/1501	_____
13. South Twin	NH	4902/1494	_____
14. Whiteface	NY	4865/1483	_____
15. Iroquois	NY	4849/1478	_____
16. Dix	NY	4839/1470*	_____
17. Carter Dome	NH	4832/1473	_____
18. Gray	NY	4826/1471	_____
19. Basin	NY	4826/1471	_____
20. Moosilauke	NH	4802/1464	_____
21. Eisenhower	NH	4761/1451	_____
22. North Twin	NH	4761/1451	_____
23. Katahdin/Hamlin	ME	4751/1605	_____
24. Gothics	NY	4734/1443	_____
25. Colden	NY	4715/1437	_____
26. Bond	NH	4698/1432	_____
27. Carrigain	NH	4780/1426	_____
28. Giant	NY	4626/1410	_____
29. Middle Carter	NH	4610/1405*	_____
30. Nippletop	NY	4609/1400*	_____
31. Santanoni	NY	4606/1404	_____
32. Redfield	NY	4606/1404	_____
33. Wright	NY	4587/1398	_____
34. West Bond	NH	4540/1384*	_____
35. Saddleback	NY	4528/1380	_____

36. Garfield	NH	4500/1372*	_____
37. Liberty	NH	4459/1359	_____
38. Armstrong	NY	4445/1350*	_____
39. Panther	NY	4442/1354	_____
40. South Carter	NH	4430/1350*	_____
41. Wildcat	NH	4422/1348	_____
42. Tabletop	NY	4413/1345	_____
43. Hough	NY	4409/1344	_____
44. Hancock, North	NH	4403/1342	_____
45. Mansfield	VT	4393/1339	_____
46. Macomb	NY	4390/1338	_____
47. Rocky Peak Ridge	NY	4383/1336	_____
48. Marshall	NY	4379/1330*	_____
49. South Kinsman	NH	4358/1328	_____
50. Allen	NY	4347/1325	_____
51. Seward	NY	4347/1320*	_____
52. Osceola	NH	4340/1323*	_____
53. Flume	NH	4328/1319	_____
54. Field	NH	4326/1319	_____
55. Pierce (Clinton)	NH	4310/1314	_____
56. Willey	NH	4302/1311	_____
57. North Kinsman	NH	4293/1309	_____
58. South Hancock	NH	4274/1302	_____
59. Bondcliff	NH	4265/1300	_____
60. Zealand	NH	4260/1298*	_____
61. Sugarloaf	ME	4250/1295*	_____
62. Big Slide	NY	4248/1290*	_____
63. Esther	NY	4239/1292	_____
64. Killington	VT	4235/1291	_____
65. Upper Wolf Jaw	NY	4203/1281	_____
66. Slide	NY(CAT)	4180/1274	_____
67. Old Speck	ME	4180/1274	_____
68. Lower Wolf Jaw	NY	4173/1272	_____
69. Cabot	NH	4170/1271*	_____
70. Crocker	ME	4168/1270	_____
71. Phelps	NY	4160/1268	_____
72. East Osceola	NH	4156/1267	_____
73. Bigelow, W. Peak	ME	4150/1265	_____
74. Sawteeth	NY	4150/1260*	_____
75. Street	NY	4150/1260*	_____

#	Name	State	Elev.	
76.	North Brother	ME	4143/1263	_____
77.	North Tripyramid	NH	4140/1262	_____
78.	Saddleback	ME	4116/1255	_____
79.	Middle Tripyramid	NH	4110/1253	_____
80.	Donaldson	NY	4108/1252	_____
81.	Cannon	NH	4100/1250*	_____
82.	Cascade	NY	4098/1249	_____
83.	Seymour	NY	4091/1247	_____
84.	Bigelow, Avery Pk	ME	4088/1246	_____
85.	Colvin	NY	4084/1240*	_____
86.	Porter	NY	4084/1240*	_____
87.	South Dix	NY	4084/1240*	_____
88.	Camel's Hump	VT	4083/1244	_____
89.	Ellen	VT	4083/1244	_____
90.	Passaconaway	NH	4060/1237	_____
91.	Hale	NH	4054/1236	_____
92.	Jackson	NH	4052/1236	_____
93.	Abraham	ME	4049/1234	_____
94.	Moriah	NH	4049/1234	_____
95.	Tom	NH	4047/1234	_____
96.	Wildcat E	NH	4041/1232	_____
97.	Hunter	NY(CAT)	4040/1231	_____
98.	Emmons	NY	4039/1231	_____
99.	Owl's Head	NH	4025/1227	_____
100.	Galehead	NH	4024/1227	_____
101.	Saddleback, Horn	ME	4023/1226	_____
102.	Dial	NY	4019/1220*	_____
103.	South Crocker	ME	4010/1222*	_____
104.	Whiteface	NH	4010/1222*	_____
105.	Abraham	VT	4006/1221	_____
106.	East Dix	NY	4006/1221	_____
107.	Waumbek	NH	4006/1221	_____
108.	Isolation	NH	4005/1221	_____
109.	Tecumseh	NH	4003/1220	_____
110.	Spaulding	ME	3988/1215	_____
111.	Blake	NY	3986/1210*	_____
112.	Readington	ME	3984/1214	_____
113.	MacNaughton	NY	3983/1214	_____
114.	Black Dome	NY(CAT)	3980/1213	_____
115.	Green	NY	3960/1207	_____

116. Snow	ME	3960/1207	_____
117. South Brother	ME	3960/1207	_____
118. Pico Peak	VT	3957/1206	_____
119. Cliff	NY	3944/1202	_____
120. Blackhead	NY(CAT)	3940/1201	_____
121. Thomas Cole	NY(CAT)	3940/1201	_____
122. Stratton	VT	3936/1200	_____
123. Nye	NY	3887/1180*	_____
124. Couchsachraga	NY	3793/1156	_____

* Elevations based on estimates from contour intervals. See Adirondack and White Mountain listings for explanation.

(CAT) = Catskills. All other summits listed under NY are located in the Adirondacks.

Notes

Notes

Notes

Other Products from New England Cartographics

Maps

Holyoke Range State Park (Eastern Section)
Holyoke Range/Skinner State Park (Western Section)
Mt. Greylock Reservation Trail Map
Mt. Toby Reservation Trail Map
Mt. Wachusett and Leominster State Forest Trail Map
Western Mass. Trail Map Pack (includes above 6 maps)
Quabbin Reservation Guide   (available in waterproof version)
New England Trails (general locator map)
Grand Monadnock Trail Map
Connecticut River Map (in Massachusetts)
Mt. Tom Reservation Trail Map
Wapack Trail Map

Books

Guide to the Taconic Trail System (in Berkshire County, MA)
Guide to the Metacomet-Monadnock Trail
Hiking the Pioneer Valley (20 circuit hikes)
The Deerfield River Guide

Send SASE for ordering information and current prices to
New England Cartographics, PO Box 9369, North Amherst,
MA 01059.

Additional copies of **High Peaks of the Northeast** can be ordered from the
publisher for $12.95 + $2.00 P & H for the first book and 75¢ for each
additional book. Telephone orders: (413) 549-4124.